SENIORS GUIDE
TO
iPhone

Monday, June 5

9:41

17

BONUS
TIPS AND TRICKS
EVERY MONTH!

Non-Tech-Savvy Step-by-Step Guide to Learn and Master All Features with Simple Instructions! | Fully Large Illustrated Guide

- SOS Mode
- Accessibility
- Siri
- Settings
- Much More!

TAILORED FOR SENIORS

TABLE OF CONTENTS

GOOD READS

Discover this and more Apps Recommended in Chapter 11

GET YOUR FREE
BOOK BONUSES NOW!

(DOWNLOAD FOR FREE WITH THE BELOW INSTRUCTION!)

FREE BONUS
UNLOCK NEW TIPS AND TRICKS EVERY SINGLE MONTH!

AMAZE YOUR FRIENDS, CHILDREN AND GRANDCHILDREN.

STAY UP-TO-DATE WITH THE BEST TIPS ON THE MARKET!

SCAN THE QR CODE BELOW AND UNLOCK THE BONUS!

INSTRUCTION ON HOW TO UNLOCK YOUR FREE BONUSES

Only 2 simple steps to unlock your free bonuses:

1) **Scan the QR code** on the previous page

2) **Let me know how you are excited about all the contents!**
I look forward to your opinion on the book and the bonus content!

SCAN THE QR CODE BELOW OR LEAVE A QUICK REVIEW ON THE AMAZON PRODUCT PAGE TO SHARE YOUR THOUGHTS ON THIS BOOK.

The best way to do it? Simple! **You can upload a brief video** with your thoughts. I will greatly appreciate an honest opinion about the book!

Don't you want to create a video? Don't worry! **You can do a short review with some photos** of dishes made thanks to this book or take photos of the most beautiful parts of the book. **Even a text-only review is appreciated!**

NOTE: You don't have to feel obligated, but it would be highly appreciated!

Scan QR Code to Leave a Review Quickly!

Introduction

The iPhone, a device that has not only redefined the smartphone sector but also revolutionized our way of life, professional engagements, and global interconnectivity. In this prelude, we embark on an expedition through the captivating annals of the iPhone's history, charting its metamorphosis from a groundbreaking innovation into a cultural icon.

The Birth of a Revolution

The inception occurred **on January 9, 2007, when the late Steve Jobs, co-founder of Apple Inc.,** graced the stage at the Macworld conference in San Francisco. Uttering the transformative words, "Today, Apple is poised to redefine the telecommunication landscape," he unveiled the inaugural iPhone. This monumental device was more than a mere telephone; it represented a visionary amalgamation of an iPod, a telecommunication apparatus, and an internet communicator. This transformative moment heralded a paradigm shift of colossal proportions.

The introduction of the iPhone in 2007 heralded a watershed juncture in the realm of technology and consumer electronics. It did not merely usher in a novel product; rather, it marked a seismic upheaval in our interface with technology. At the epicenter of this transformative epoch was the iPhone's intuitive touchscreen interface, obviating the need for physical keyboards and tactile buttons. This innovation conferred universal accessibility across generational and tech proficiency divides, casting the die for a smartphone revolution that would revolutionize industries ranging from telecommunication and photography to entertainment and productivity.

The Evolution of a Cultural Icon

Subsequent to its epochal inauguration, **the iPhone underwent a continuum of transformative evolutions, each layering advancements upon the successes and capacities of its forerunner.** The advent of the iPhone 3G in 2008 ushered in swifter internet connectivity and the inception of the App Store, catalyzing an influx of third-party applications that endowed the iPhone with unparalleled versatility for myriad applications. **Successive iterations introduced pioneering features such as FaceTime, Siri, and Touch ID, perpetually augmenting the device's capabilities and augmenting the user experience.**

Incontrovertibly, the iPhone wielded profound cultural sway, evolving into a symbol of innovation, sophistication, and aspiration. Its streamlined aesthetics, juxtaposed with Apple's gamut of services, spawned an ardent following that transcended the boundaries of tech enthusiasts. The iPhone ascended beyond the realm of a mere gadget, ingraining itself as an intrinsic facet of our quotidian existence, reshaping the mechanisms of communication, memory preservation, global navigation, and even health management.

With each novel release, the iPhone not only transgressed technological thresholds but also redrew the blueprint of our anticipations pertaining to the capabilities of a smartphone.

A Global Phenomenon

As the iPhone's evolutionary journey persisted, its global resonance burgeoned logarithmically. It transitioned from being a product predominantly accessible within select nations to an apparatus attainable to individuals across the globe. **Apple's commitment to inclusivity and adaptation translated into the iPhone's compatibility with an array of languages and seamless harmonization with diverse cultural milieus.** Its far-reaching impact on various sectors, from application developers to accessory manufacturers, precipitated the emergence of a thriving ecosystem that engendered employment and innovation on a global scale.

Moreover, the iPhone catalyzed a transformative progression within the mobile telecommunications arena. It confronted the established norms of contractual entanglements, compelling service providers to reassess their pricing methodologies. The introduction of unlocked iPhones and contract-independent acquisition choices empowered consumers with greater autonomy over their mobile experiences, fomenting competition and diversification.

The iPhone's odyssey, starting with its pioneering inception and culminating as a global cultural lodestar, serves as an ode to the potency of innovation and design. It not only metamorphosed our technological engagement but also elicited profound ramifications on society and economics. As we delve deeper into its historical trajectory, we shall traverse the significant milestones and innovations that have enshrined the iPhone as an enduring emblem of advancement and interconnectedness.

The Inaugural iPhone (2007)

The original iPhone featured a 3.5-inch display, a 2-megapixel camera, and a capacitive touch screen, which was a novelty at the time. It operated on the initial iteration of iOS, recognized as iPhone OS. Despite its constraints in comparison to modern models, the inaugural iPhone established the groundwork for what was to follow.

iPhone 3G (2008)

Just a year later, Apple presented the iPhone 3G, which brought not only 3G network support but also the App Store—a game-changing addition that allowed third-party developers to formulate applications for the iPhone. This marked the commencement of an app ecosystem that would ultimately evolve into the App Store we are acquainted with today.

iPhone 4 (2010)

The iPhone 4 was a design marvel. It showcased the Retina display, which offered an unmatched level of screen clarity at the time. This model also introduced FaceTime, revolutionizing video conversations. Its dazzling glass and stainless-steel design established a fresh benchmark for smartphone aesthetics.

iPhone 5 (2012)

With the iPhone 5, Apple persisted in its tradition of innovation. This model was the first to incorporate the lightning connector, replacing the traditional 30-pin dock connector. It was also sleeker and lighter than its forerunners, illustrating Apple's commitment to both form and function.

iPhone 6 and 6 Plus (2014)

The iPhone 6 and 6 Plus marked a notable shift in design, showcasing more extensive displays of 4.7 inches and 5.5 inches, respectively. This transition to larger screens corresponded to the demand for more substantial, more immersive displays and set the stage for the "phablet" trend.

iPhone 5

iPhone 7 and 7 Plus (2016)

The iPhone 7 and 7 Plus introduced water resistance, dual-lens cameras, and the elimination of the traditional headphone jack—a bold action that sparked debates and expedited the adoption of wireless audio.

iPhone X (2017)

The iPhone X, denoted as "iPhone Ten," commemorated the tenth anniversary of the iPhone. It boasted an edge-to-edge OLED display, Face ID facial recognition, and a departure from the iconic home button. This model marked a significant advance in design and technology.

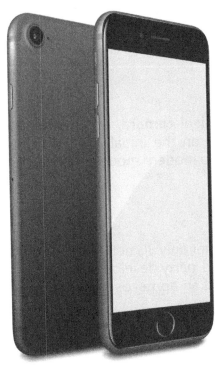

iPhone 7

iPhone XS, XS Max, and XR (2018)

These models perpetuated the iPhone X's legacy with enhanced cameras, performance, and the introduction of the iPhone XR—an economical alternative that maintained numerous of the flagship's features.

iPhone 11, 11 Pro, and 11 Pro Max (2019)

The iPhone 11 series made a powerful impression with its potent A13 Bionic chip, Night mode photography, and improved battery life. It illustrated Apple's dedication to delivering outstanding experiences to users.

iPhone 12 Series (2020)

The iPhone 12 series ushered in 5G connectivity to the iPhone lineup, making it prepared for the subsequent generation of mobile networks. Its streamlined design and MagSafe technology for accessories were notable highlights.

iPhone 13 Series (2021)

The most recent extension to the iPhone family, the iPhone 13 series, enhanced upon its forerunner with upgraded camera capabilities, extended battery life, and a faster A15 Bionic chip.

iPhone XS

The iPhone 14 Series (2022)

Building on its illustrious legacy, the iPhone 14 Series, unveiled in 2022, continued Apple's commitment to innovation and excellence. This latest installment in the iPhone family brought forth a range of noteworthy enhancements and features that further solidified its place as a leader in the smartphone market.

The iPhone 15 (Anticipated Arrival in September 2023)

The impending debut of the iPhone 15, projected to grace the market in September 2023, heralds the forthcoming stage in the evolutionary trajectory of Apple's renowned smartphone lineage. While the precise details remain veiled in secrecy until the official unveiling, we can eagerly anticipate a device that seamlessly amalgamates pioneering design, elevated display technology, formidable performance capabilities, advanced photographic functionalities, and enhanced connectivity.

In keeping with the tradition of its forerunners, the iPhone 15 is poised to redefine the parameters of smartphone accomplishments, proffering an unparalleled user experience that aligns with Apple's unwavering dedication to excellence and pioneering ingenuity. Remain attuned for forthcoming revelations concerning this anxiously awaited augmentation to the illustrious iPhone family.

A Legacy of Innovation

From its modest beginnings, the iPhone has evolved into a symbol of ingenuity and distinction. It has transcended its role as a mere communication device, evolving into an indispensable aspect of our lives. As we delve into the iPhone's attributes and functionalities in this book, we pay tribute to its remarkable history and honor the assurance of what's to come. The iPhone journey persists, and we're thrilled to have you on board.

iPhone 15 PRO

Glossary

Traversing the realm of smartphones, including the renowned iPhone, might feel somewhat daunting, especially given the abundance of technical terminology. This glossary serves as your dependable companion, elucidating fundamental expressions and notions that are vital to your smartphone involvement. From connectivity to hardware and software attributes, grasping these expressions will empower you to maximize your iPhone's potential.

1. **Wi-Fi (Wireless Fidelity)**: Wi-Fi stands as a wireless networking technology that enables your iPhone to connect to the internet and other devices sans the need for physical cables. It constitutes the bedrock for browsing, streaming, and downloading apps and content.

2. **Bluetooth**: Bluetooth signifies a wireless technology that facilitates your iPhone's connection to other proximate devices, such as headphones, speakers, and smartwatches. It lies at the heart of wireless audio and accessory linkage.

3. **Location Services**: Location Services utilize GPS, Wi-Fi, and cellular data to ascertain your iPhone's whereabouts. This aspect is indispensable for mapping, navigation apps, and location-oriented services.

4. **Cellular Data**: Cellular data affords your iPhone the capability to link up with the internet via your mobile carrier's network. It proves crucial for web surfing, messaging, and accessing online content in situations where Wi-Fi is unavailable.

5. **App Store**: The App Store serves as Apple's digital marketplace, where you can peruse, retrieve, and update apps and games for your iPhone. It serves as a repository of software catering to every requirement and interest.

6. **iOS (iPhone Operating System)**: iOS operates as the operating system steering your iPhone. It garners recognition for its user-friendly interface, routine updates, and security attributes.

7. **Siri**: Siri acts as Apple's virtual assistant. Activation may occur through voice commands or a button press, and it boasts the ability to answer queries, establish reminders, dispatch messages, and control assorted functions on your iPhone.

8. **Face ID and Touch ID**: Face ID (on newer models) and Touch ID (on older models) signify biometric authentication methods. These facilitate unlocking your iPhone, executing secure payments, and accessing apps and data via your face or fingerprint.

9. **iCloud**: iCloud represents Apple's cloud storage and synchronization service. It empowers you to back up your iPhone, gain access to your photos, documents, and data from other Apple devices, and share content with others.

10. **App Permissions**: Apps on your iPhone might solicit diverse permissions, encompassing access to your camera, microphone, or location. Management of these permissions is feasible through your iPhone's settings.

11. AirDrop: AirDrop embodies a feature that permits wireless exchange of photos, videos, documents, and additional files with neighboring Apple devices. It leverages Bluetooth and Wi-Fi for expeditious and secure transfers.

12. Notifications: Notifications keep you apprised of fresh messages, app updates, and events. Tailoring notification settings for each app furnishes control over what appears on your lock screen.

13. VPN (Virtual Private Network): A VPN designates a service that enhances your online privacy and security. It encrypts your internet connection, rendering it more arduous for others to intercept your data.

14. Dark Mode: Dark Mode signifies a display alternative that transforms the color palette of your iPhone's interface to incorporate darker hues. It not only pleases aesthetically but may also alleviate eye strain in low-light environments.

15. Control Center: The Control Center confers swift access to critical settings and functionalities, encompassing screen brightness, volume, Wi-Fi, and Bluetooth toggles. Invocation involves a downward swipe from the top-right corner of the screen.

16. Multitasking: Multitasking facilitates the seamless transition between apps, operation of apps in the background, and employment of split-screen or picture-in-picture mode to enhance productivity.

17. Safari: Safari represents Apple's web browser. It delivers a prompt and secure browsing experience, replete with features such as tab management, private browsing, and password autofill.

18. Widgets: Widgets amount to interactive, customizable elements that supply immediate information or expedited access to app functions. Inclusion of widgets on your iPhone's home screen is achievable.

19. AirPods: AirPods are Apple's wireless earbuds. They offer effortless integration with your iPhone, delivering high-quality audio and hands-free Siri interaction.

20. Animoji and Memoji: Animoji denote animated emoji characters that mirror your facial expressions via the iPhone's TrueDepth camera. Memoji manifest as personalized animated avatars fashioned after your visage.

21. FaceTime: FaceTime embodies Apple's video and audio calling service, enabling high-quality video conversations with other Apple devices. It proves ideal for maintaining connections with loved ones.

22. AirPlay: AirPlay embodies a feature that empowers the streaming of audio and video from your iPhone to compatible devices, such as Apple TV and AirPlay-enabled speakers.

23. Control Center: The Control Center confers swift access to critical settings and functionalities, encompassing screen brightness, volume, Wi-Fi, and Bluetooth toggles. Invocation involves a downward swipe from the top-right corner of the screen.

24. Multitasking: Multitasking facilitates the seamless transition between apps, operation of apps in the background, and employment of split-screen or picture-in-picture mode to enhance productivity.

25. Safari: Safari represents Apple's web browser. It delivers a prompt and secure browsing experience, replete with features such as tab management, private browsing, and password autofill.

26. Widgets: Widgets amount to interactive, customizable elements that supply immediate information or expedited access to app functions. Inclusion of widgets on your iPhone's home screen is achievable.

27. AirPods: AirPods are Apple's wireless earbuds. They offer effortless integration with your iPhone, delivering high-quality audio and hands-free Siri interaction.

28. Animoji and Memoji: Animoji denote animated emoji characters that mirror your facial expressions via the iPhone's TrueDepth camera. Memoji manifest as personalized animated avatars fashioned after your visage.

29. iCloud Drive: iCloud Drive represents a cloud storage service that enables the storage and synchronization of files, documents, and photos across all your Apple devices. It stands as your virtual file repository in the cloud.

30. Night Mode: Night Mode stands as a camera attribute enhancing low-light photography. It automatically adjusts exposure and captures exquisite photos even in dimly illuminated surroundings.

31. Do Not Disturb: Do Not Disturb constitutes a feature that suppresses calls, notifications, and alerts during designated intervals. It proves optimal for uninterrupted concentration or serene nocturnal repose.

32. QR Codes: QR (Quick Response) codes amount to scannable codes capable of encompassing links, information, or contact particulars. Your iPhone's camera possesses the ability to scan QR codes, facilitating prompt access to websites or information.

33. Battery Health: Battery Health represents a feature empowering you to monitor and optimize your iPhone's battery performance. It provides insights into battery capacity and peak performance capability.

34. Find My iPhone: Find My iPhone acts as a security feature aiding in the localization of your misplaced or stolen iPhone. Additionally, it grants the ability to remotely lock or erase your device to safeguard your data.

35. App Tracking Transparency: App Tracking Transparency amounts to a privacy feature mandating apps to solicit your consent prior to tracking your activity across other apps and websites.

Equipping yourself with comprehension of these prevalent iPhone and smartphone expressions resembles unveiling the enigma of an extensive realm of possibilities. As you delve further into your iPhone expedition, this glossary shall serve as your compass to decipher the intricacies of your device and optimize its attributes and capabilities.

Chapter 1:

Getting Started with the iPhone 🎤

Welcome to the extraordinary universe of the iPhone, a device that has revolutionized the manner in which we communicate, labor, and amuse ourselves. Whether you're a novice iPhone proprietor or in the process of upgrading to the most recent model, this chapter functions as your guiding star, leading you through the exhilarating initiation process, vital configurations, and the indispensable Apple ID. We will also delve into the groundbreaking Emergency SOS feature, a potential life-saver.

Initial setup and basic settings

Visualize the moment of unveiling your new iPhone as the act of unlocking a gateway to a realm brimming with possibilities. Here's your blueprint for initiating a seamless commencement:

1. Unboxing your iPhone

Unveiling the contents of your fresh iPhone package is akin to the act of unearthing a portal to a realm characterized by innovation and potential. Apple's scrupulous devotion to minutiae shines as you lift the cover of the sleek box.

The instant your gaze falls upon your new iPhone, you'll be able to discern the design, precision, and artistry that have forged Apple into an iconic brand. Savor this instant at your leisure, making sure you've uncovered everything enclosed within the packaging – your iPhone, charging cord, adapter, and perhaps even a set of EarPods. These accompanying accessories have been thoughtfully selected to complement your iPhone experience, with each component meticulously chosen to augment your journey.

Pro tip: Maintain the condition of the box and the packaging materials. If, at some point, you decide to sell or trade in your iPhone, the presence of the original packaging can enhance its resale value.

2. Powering on

After you've unboxed your iPhone, it is time to breathe life into it. Identify the power button, usually situated on the right side or the top of the device, depending on the iPhone model. Depress and hold this button until the iconic Apple logo gracefully materializes on the screen.

This moment symbolizes the commencement of your iPhone's digital pulse. As the system initializes, you'll be joining millions of users across the globe in a digital odyssey that links individuals, knowledge, and experiences. The sight of the Apple logo stands as a testament to the potency of technology in shaping our lives and interactions.

> *Pro Tip: If your iPhone fails to power on, ensure it's charged. Attach it to a power source using the provided charger and cord, then repeat the power-on procedure.*

3. Language and Region

Your iPhone is a device that adapts itself to your predilections, and the preliminary setup is where it all commences. The process of selecting language and region guarantees that your device communicates in your preferred tongue, displays time and date formats accurately, and aligns itself with your geographic location. Elect your favored language from the list of available alternatives and then designate your region or country.

This selection governs your iPhone's behavior in numerous ways, including the language it employs, the currency it exhibits, and even the format of date presentations. These seemingly straightforward choices personalize your iPhone, metamorphosing it into an extension of your identity and a device that genuinely comprehends your needs.

> *Pro Tip: If you frequently travel or live in a multilingual household, don't fret; you can adjust these settings at your leisure in your iPhone's preferences. Your iPhone has been designed to be adaptable and versatile, accommodating shifts in circumstances.*

4. Connect to Wi-Fi

At this juncture, your iPhone has powered on, and you've made selections regarding language and region. It's now time to forge a connection with a Wi-Fi network. The act of linking up with Wi-Fi is of paramount importance during the preliminary setup.

Though your iPhone can operate using cellular data, Wi-Fi offers a swifter and more stable connection, an essential prerequisite for an effortless initiation. Direct your attention to the Wi-Fi network you wish to join, input the network password if necessary, and your iPhone will establish a connection. This step ascertains that your device can effortlessly procure updates, apps, and other imperative data during the setup process. It's a moment of great significance, for Wi-Fi connectivity lays the groundwork for your iPhone's online journey.

Pro Tip: If you're performing the iPhone setup in an area devoid of Wi-Fi accessibility, you can proceed by utilizing cellular data. Nevertheless, exercise prudence in managing data usage, especially if your data plan has limitations.

5. Quick Start (Optional)

In the event that you're transitioning from a prior iPhone or transferring data from another Apple device, the Quick Start feature presents itself as your gateway to a seamless shift. Quick Start obviates the necessity for manual data migration and configuration of settings. Merely adhere to the on-screen directives and position your former device in close proximity to your new iPhone.

Your fresh iPhone will recognize your previous device and prompt you to configure your new device with your extant Apple ID, preferences, and settings. It's akin to the effortless transference of your digital existence, guaranteeing that you experience no disruption as you make the transition to your new iPhone. This functionality underscores the convenience and innovation that Apple brings to the user experience.

Pro Tip: For an optimal outcome, both devices must run iOS 11 or later and have Bluetooth enabled. Ascertain that your former device remains charged and linked to a stable Wi-Fi network for the best results.

6. Setting Up Face ID or Touch ID

Present-day iPhones often boast either **Face ID or Touch ID**, **offering secure and convenient modes of authentication.** The establishment of one of these biometric options enhances the security and usability of your iPhone. Should your iPhone support Face ID, adhere to the on-screen prompts to capture scans of your visage from assorted angles.

In the case of devices equipped with Touch ID, you'll be prompted to record the fingerprint of your choosing by positioning your finger on the designated sensor. These technologies ensure that your device can solely be unlocked by you, granting access to your confidential data. Biometric authentication is not solely secure but also convenient, abolishing the requirement to remember intricate passcodes.

> *Pro Tip: To increase convenience, consider registering more than a single fingerprint or facial scan. You have the option to add an alternative appearance or fingerprint, a useful provision in scenarios where you wear glasses or exhibit variations in visage due to alterations in hairstyle.*

7. Craft a Secure Passcode

Although biometrics deliver exemplary security, the formulation of a secure passcode serves as an additional stratum of safeguarding. Your passcode operates as a backup mechanism for unlocking your iPhone or authenticating sensitive actions. **It's imperative that you create a passcode that isn't easily guessable.**

Shun commonplace combinations such as "1234" or "0000." Instead, conceive of an exclusive code recognized solely by you. A secure passcode confers supplementary protection to your device, certifying that even if someone attains physical possession of it, they cannot infringe upon your privacy unbeknownst to you.

> *Pro Tip: For augmented security, contemplate configuring complex alphanumeric passcodes. This entails navigating to Settings > Face ID & Passcode (or Touch ID & Passcode), then electing "Change Passcode." Subsequently, choose "Passcode Options" and opt for "Custom Alphanumeric Code."*

8. Restore Content from iCloud or iTunes (Optional)

If you're upgrading from a previous iPhone or have an existing iCloud or iTunes backup, this step allows you to seamlessly transfer your data, apps, and settings to your new device. It's tantamount to resurrecting your digital realm upon the novel canvas of your iPhone.

You can elect to restore from either an iCloud backup or an iTunes backup, contingent on your preferences and circumstances. iCloud backups bestow the convenience of accessibility from any location furnished with an internet connection, while iTunes backups are consigned to local storage on your computer. The act of restoration guarantees that your contacts, photographs, messages, applications, and additional data find their way to your fresh iPhone, thereby economizing both your time and endeavor.

> *Pro Tip: Make it a routine to periodically execute backups of your preceding device via iCloud or iTunes. This measure ensures the availability of a recent backup when the time arises to set up a new iPhone, preserving your data and configurations.*

9. Sign In with Your Apple ID

Your Apple ID serves as the master key for unlocking a realm brimming with Apple services and functionalities. The process of signing in with your Apple ID entwines your iPhone with the intricate tapestry of the Apple ecosystem, encompassing the App Store, iCloud, iMessage, FaceTime, and beyond. In the event that you already possess an Apple ID, simply furnish your Apple ID email and password.

In the absence of one, you possess the option to craft an Apple ID during the setup process. It's imperative to etch your Apple ID credentials into your memory, for they furnish ingress to your digital existence across an array of devices. Your Apple ID guarantees the seamless synchronization of your iPhone with your remaining Apple devices, facilitating the resumption of tasks across different platforms, be it on your iPhone, iPad, or Mac.

Pro Tip: Elevate the security of your Apple ID by instituting two-factor authentication (2FA). Through 2FA, even if an unauthorized party gains knowledge of your password, access to your account is unattainable without a supplementary form of verification.

10. Set Up iCloud Settings:

iCloud stands as the backbone of your iPhone's cloud-based services. **It confers secure storage for your photographs, videos, documents, application data, and more, thereby rendering them accessible across all your Apple devices.** In the course of setup, you have the prerogative to designate the components you wish to synchronize with iCloud. This encompassment extends to alternatives such as iCloud Drive, Photos, Contacts, Calendars, and additional facets.

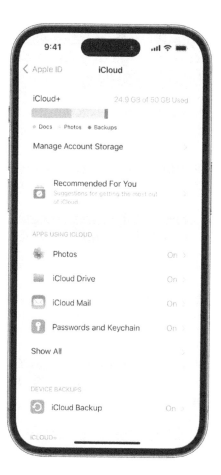

The activation of iCloud services safeguards your data, rendering it recoverable in cases where your device faces misplacement, and assuring perpetual alignment with the most up-to-date iterations. Beyond this, iCloud streamlines the process of sharing files, photographs, and documents with friends and family. It stands as an integral segment of the Apple ecosystem, orchestrating the organization and accessibility of your digital existence.

Pro Tip: Should apprehensions regarding iCloud storage limitations permeate your thoughts, ponder the feasibility of upgrading to an expanded storage plan. This ensures the availability of sufficient space for your photographs, videos, and backups.

11. Set Up Siri (Optional):

Siri, your virtual assistant, remains perpetually poised to aid you with tasks, dispense answers to inquiries, and furnish customized suggestions. In the event that you elect to activate Siri during the initiation process, you will be steered through the procedure of configuring your voice assistant.

Siri acclimates to your vocal timbre and preferences, evolving into an invaluable instrument for hands-free interactions. The customization of Siri's comportment is likewise feasible, encompassing the selection of your preferred voice and the establishment of **"Hey Siri"** for voice-triggered assistance. The capabilities of Siri continue to burgeon with each iOS update, solidifying its stature as a formidable and indispensable facet of your iPhone.

Pro Tip: Extract the maximum utility from Siri by delving into its array of commands and integrations with applications. Siri can convey messages, set reminders, supply directions, and even exercise control over smart home contraptions.

12. Set Up Apple Pay (Optional):

Apple Pay effectuates a revolution in the realm of payment methods by permitting the secure storage of your credit and debit cards upon your iPhone. This affords the opportunity for swift, contactless transactions at vendors that extend support, both in brick-and-mortar establishments and in the digital arena. To institute Apple Pay, append your cards to the Wallet application and execute the requisite verification process. Following this configuration, you will be endowed with the capability to utilize Apple Pay at terminals furnished with NFC technology, or alternatively, for online purchases conducted within applications and on websites. Apple Pay epitomizes a convenient, secure, and private approach to executing transactions, obviating the need to tote about physical cards.

Pro Tip: The security inherent to Apple Pay extends not solely to protection but also to privacy. The veritable numbers of your cards never repose within your device or Apple's servers, thus ensuring the confidentiality of your financial information.

13. Customize Your Display & Brightness Settings:

The display of your iPhone is the portal to the digital cosmos, and the personalization of its attributes to align with your preferences is of paramount importance. **In this phase, you possess the liberty to adjust parameters such as Brightness, Text Size, and Display Zoom.**

If you harbor a penchant for a somber user interface, you possess the capability to activate Dark Mode, which serves to alleviate ocular strain in environments characterized by subdued illumination. You are also entitled to vary the dimensions and style of text to facilitate facile perusal. Features such as True Tone function to adapt the display in accordance with ambient lighting conditions, thus bestowing a more naturalistic viewing experience. The configuration of your display settings serves to ensure the comfort and felicity of your interaction with your iPhone.

Pro Tip: Consider the activation of Auto-Brightness to enable your iPhone to autonomously regulate screen luminosity in accordance with ambient surroundings, thereby optimizing both visibility and battery life.

14. Customize Your Sounds & Haptics Settings:

Your iPhone extends a plethora of customization alternatives in the realm of sounds and haptic feedback. **In this juncture, you are entitled to calibrate your ringtone, text notification tone, and vibration settings to reflect your individualistic style.** You can even conceive custom vibration patterns that pertain to specific contacts.

These settings guarantee your ability to promptly discern incoming calls, messages, and notifications, whether through a cursory glance or by virtue of subtle vibrations. The personalization of sounds and haptics serves to infuse a distinctive imprint upon your device, thereby rendering it uniquely and unmistakably your own.

> *Pro Tip: Configure distinct vibration patterns for varying notifications to enable facile differentiation between alerts sans the necessity of scrutinizing your device. For instance, it is plausible to configure an elongated vibration for messages and a truncated one for emails.*

15. Choose Your Wallpaper:

Your ability to personalize the home screen of your iPhone lies within the selection of the perfect wallpaper. Apple endows you with an assemblage of captivating wallpapers, incorporating dynamic and live selections among others. You possess the latitude to select from a manifold assortment of genres, ranging from depictions of nature to instances of abstract artistry. The choice of a wallpaper that resonates with your sensibilities does not solely enhance the aesthetic allure of your device but also confers upon it an aura of being an extension of your character. You hold the option to further tweak your chosen wallpaper by dictating whether it assumes a presence on the lock screen, home screen, or both.

> *Pro Tip: Engage in periodic alternations of your wallpaper to infuse a sense of novelty and excitement into the appearance of your device. Additionally, the configuration of dynamic wallpapers, which subtly shift with the motion of your device, infuses an element of dynamism into your screen.*

16. Customize Your Home Screen:

The home screen of your iPhone serves as the portal through which you access your most frequently employed applications and widgets. This juncture presents the occasion to organize your applications by way of relocation about the screen, the formation of folders for their organization, and the incorporation of widgets for at-a-glance access to information.

The act of personalizing your home screen assures that your most critical tools are readily accessible, and your device functions in alignment with your proclivities. The home screen of your iPhone is akin to a digital canvas, and you hold the position of the artist vested with the prerogative to determine both its appearance and functionality.

> *Pro Tip: Exploit the App Library feature to effectuate the automatic organization of applications into categories, thereby preserving a clean and uncluttered home screen.*

17. Privacy & Security Settings:

The sanctity of your privacy and security remains an utmost priority, and Apple bequeaths a robust suite of tools to shield your personal information. In this phase, you possess the liberty to peruse and fine-tune an array of privacy settings. The decisions made in this domain include the sharing of analytic data with Apple, the governance of location access for applications, and the management of permissions pertaining to camera and microphone access.

The activation of features such as Find My iPhone heightens the security of your device, facilitating the task of locating it in the event of loss or theft. It is prudent to dedicate sufficient time to the scrutiny of these settings and the selection of those that resonate with your comfort level.

> *Pro Tip: Prudently conduct periodic reviews of your application permissions to ensure that solely trusted applications are accorded access to sensitive data such as location, photos, and contacts.*

18. Sign Into Your Email Accounts:

The management of your email accounts assumes the guise of an effortless endeavor upon your iPhone, be it via Apple's native Mail application or third-party email clients.

The process entails the provisioning of your email addresses and corresponding passwords, a course of action that results in the automatic configuration of your email accounts, guaranteeing the seamless receipt of messages devoid of undue complication.

Your email accounts will be conveniently accessible through the Mail application, wherein you can undertake the sending, reception, and organization of your emails sans impediment.

> *Pro Tip: Institute email notifications to ensure the receipt of critical messages without succumbing to the inundation of incessant notifications.*

The Importance of the Apple ID

Your Apple ID stands as the linchpin of the Apple ecosystem, bridging the chasm between your device and an array of Apple services and functionalities:

- **App Store Access**: Your Apple ID grants you passage to the App Store, an abundant repository of applications, games, and content. It functions as a meticulous keeper of your acquisitions and simplifies the process of downloading your favored applications across a multitude of devices.

App Store

- **iCloud Storage**: iCloud furnishes secure storage for your photos, videos, documents, and backups. Your Apple ID serves as your gateway to the administration and access of your iCloud data from any geographical location.

- **Find My iPhone Security**: In instances where your iPhone encounters loss or theft, your Apple ID confers the power to remotely ascertain its location, instigate a locking mechanism, or even effectuate its erasure via the Find My iPhone feature.

Find My

- **Seamless Communication**: FaceTime, iMessage, and a sundry assortment of communication services lean upon your Apple ID for the establishment of connections with acquaintances and family members spanning the globe. Your Apple ID assures the synchronization of your messages and calls across your repertoire of Apple devices.

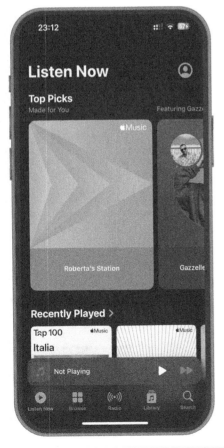

Music

- **Apple Music Harmony**: If you harbor a passion for music, your Apple ID delivers entry to the extensive library of Apple Music. It avails you the opportunity to explore, stream, and download millions of tracks and playlists.

- **Cross-Device Continuity**: Your Apple ID interconnects your iPhone with a medley of supplementary Apple devices, encompassing your iPad, Mac, Apple Watch, and beyond. This harmonious interlinking permits the commencement of tasks on one device and their seamless continuation on another.

Pro Tip: Safeguard your Apple ID with the diligence afforded to a prized possession. Employ a robust and unique password, activate two-factor authentication (2FA), and engage in periodic reviews of your account activity to pinpoint any irregular signs of access.

How to set up and use the emergency SOS feature

Your iPhone transcends its role as a mere communications and entertainment device; it metamorphoses into a lifeline during times of crisis. The Emergency SOS feature has been meticulously devised to summon aid in the moments when it is needed most:

1. **Activation of Emergency SOS**: The initiation of Emergency SOS entails the simultaneous depression of the side button (located on the right side of your iPhone) and one of the volume buttons. This gesture brings forth a slider that sanctions the placement of an emergency call.

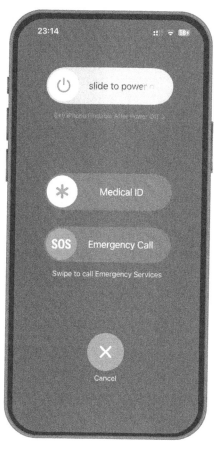 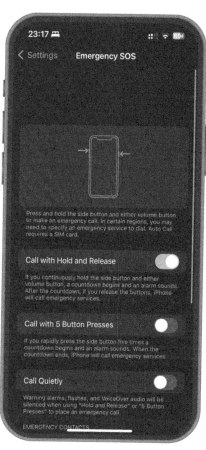

2. **Automatic SOS Activation**: In instances where the side button and volume buttons are held down continuously for a defined duration without interruption, your iPhone enters an automated SOS mode. This is characterized by the commencement of a countdown and the subsequent automatic placement of an emergency call to your designated emergency contacts or local authorities.

3. **Provision of Emergency Information**: Your iPhone enables you to supply pertinent emergency information that can be invaluable to responders. This information encompasses

your medical conditions, allergies, blood type, and organ donor status. It additionally facilitates the incorporation of emergency contacts who can be notified in times of crisis. These details are accessed by means of the Medical ID feature within the Health application.

4.   Emergency Contacts: Upon the activation of Emergency SOS, your iPhone has the potential to notify your designated emergency contacts by means of a message conveying your current location and the impending emergency. These contacts are also sent updates should your location change.

5.   Alarm and Flashlight Activation: Emergency SOS activates the alarm and flashlight on your iPhone to both attract attention and serve as aids in low-light situations.

Pro Tip: Familiarize yourself with the functionality of Emergency SOS and impart knowledge of its operation to your acquaintances and family members. It stands as a potentially life-saving feature in situations where immediate intervention is imperative.

With your iPhone now initialized and an array of personalizations executed, your journey in the realm of Apple technology commences in earnest. This device serves as your loyal companion, your conduit to the digital universe, and your enabler for countless endeavors. In the forthcoming chapters, we shall traverse the facets of iPhone usage, delving into communication, productivity, creativity, entertainment, and security.

Remember, your iPhone is not merely a device; it is your digital emissary, poised to facilitate your desires and aspirations in ways that stretch the boundaries of possibility. May your expedition with this remarkable gadget be marked by both delight and revelation as you explore the boundless vistas it unfurls before you.

Chapter 2:

2.1 Wallpapers and Ringtones

Changing Wallpaper and Ringtones

The journey of personalizing your iPhone starts with the customization of its visual and auditory aspects. Changing your wallpaper is akin to giving your iPhone a fresh, aesthetic makeover. **To embark on this endeavor, navigate to the "Settings" on your iPhone and select the "Wallpaper" option.**

 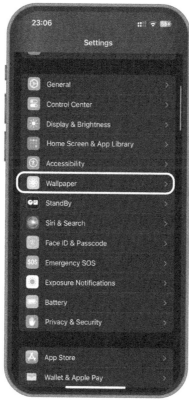 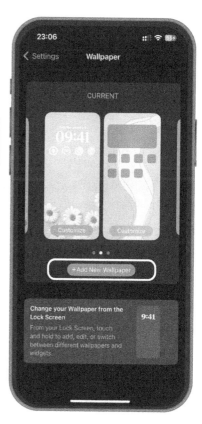

Here, you have the choice to explore Apple's meticulously designed default wallpapers or employ your own photos as your wallpaper. Whether you opt for a serene landscape, a cherished memory, or a vibrant work of art, your choice of wallpaper sets the stage for making your iPhone truly unique and reflective of your personality.

Pro Tip: Elevate your visual experience by selecting wallpapers that not only look great but also resonate with your personal style.

Change Ringtone

Diversifying your ringtones is another avenue of personalization that adds an element of fun. **To begin, navigate to "Settings," access "Sounds & Haptics," and explore the "Ringtone" section.** Here, you'll find a variety of pre-installed ringtones. However, you need not limit yourself to these options.

You have the freedom to use custom ringtones, allowing you to set your favorite song, a meaningful melody, or even a playful sound as your unique ringtone. This step adds an auditory dimension that makes your iPhone truly distinctive.

For an extra touch, you can even assign custom ringtones to specific contacts, instantly identifying incoming calls without needing to glance at your screen.

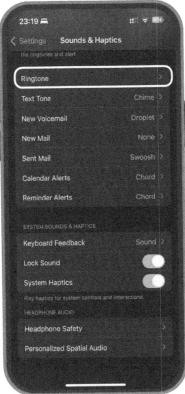

Pro Tip: Choose ringtones that align with your auditory preferences and have the power to bring a smile to your face, giving your iPhone a touch of personality that reflects your identity.

Notification Sounds

Your iPhone offers a myriad of ways to further tailor your auditory experience. In addition to changing your ringtone, you can also customize notification sounds. **To do this, navigate to "Settings," then "Sounds & Haptics."** In this section, you'll find various options to adjust notification sounds for different events such as new emails, text messages, and calendar events. Selecting distinct sounds for various notifications can help you easily identify the nature of incoming alerts, allowing for a more efficient response.

> *Pro Tip: Customize notification sounds to suit your preferences and prioritize important alerts with unique and recognizable tones.*

Ringtone Volume and Silent/Vibration Mode

Ensuring that your iPhone adapts seamlessly to your surroundings is essential. This is where managing ringtone volume and utilizing the silent/vibrate mode becomes crucial. In situations like meetings or quiet environments, a sudden loud ringtone can be disruptive. Adjusting the ringtone volume is a straightforward task. **The physical buttons on the side of your iPhone allow you to quickly increase or decrease the volume to your preferred level. A simple press of the volume-up or volume-down button does the job.**

Silent mode, on the other hand, comes to the rescue when audible ringing would be disruptive or inappropriate. Located just above the volume buttons on your iPhone is a convenient switch. When you move this switch to the silent position, indicated by the orange color, your iPhone becomes peacefully quiet – no ringing or buzzing. However, this doesn't mean you'll miss important calls or notifications. With silent mode activated, your iPhone will discreetly vibrate for calls and notifications, ensuring you stay connected without causing any disturbances.

2.2 Managing Notifications

How notifications work

In the contemporary landscape of interconnectivity, the acquisition of timely information assumes paramount importance. Your iPhone emerges as an adept purveyor of real-time updates, extending them directly to your grasp. Notifications serve as the lifeblood of this experience. These notifications encapsulate momentous messages from your applications, efficiently showcased

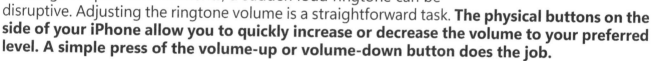

on your lock screen, within the confines of the Notification Center, or even as unobtrusive banners during your active usage of the iPhone. Visualize them as succinct missives from your applications, conveniently on display to keep you abreast of a myriad of events, encompassing text messages, emails, social media interactions, and news bulletins. Notifications epitomize your iPhone's commitment to preserving your awareness, and they remain malleable to cater to your preferences.

Pro Tip: Cultivate the habit of perusing your notifications consistently to remain well-informed and to facilitate prompt responses.

Customizing notifications for specific apps

Not all notifications merit equal significance, and your iPhone acknowledges this reality. You are conferred with the authority to assume the role of a digital gatekeeper, determining which applications are authorized to dispatch notifications and how these notifications manifest.

This granular level of control assumes critical importance in preserving the harmony of your digital existence. **To access this suite of customization options, embark on a sojourn to your iPhone's "Settings" and progress to the "Notifications" domain.**

Here, an array of your installed applications awaits, each accompanied by a distinct set of notification parameters. **It falls upon your discretion to dictate which applications are authorized to produce sounds, unveil banners, or secure a place within the Notification Center.** This paradigm bestows upon you a semblance of being the conductor of a digital orchestra, ensuring that solely the most pivotal notes reach your auditory faculties.

> *Pro Tip: Afford precedence to notifications originating from indispensable applications such as messaging or calendar applications to streamline your digital interaction.*

How to silence notifications during the night or important events

The world, as you are well aware, continues its perpetual revolution, even during your hours of repose or when you are ensconced in pivotal events. Your iPhone, in a manner reminiscent of its ceaseless activity, need not disrupt moments of leisure or importance. A straightforward remedy resides in the form of **"Do Not Disturb."**

This ingenious feature empowers you to establish specific timeframes during which your iPhone will effectuate the automatic suppression of notifications, thereby guaranteeing the preservation of your tranquility during moments of paramount significance.

To set "Do Not Disturb" into motion, navigate to the "Settings" and engage with the dedicated section.

Within this precinct, you may designate hours of placidity, create exceptions for specific contacts, or activate the **"Bedtime" mode**, an option that orchestrates the gradual dimming of your screen and the silencing of notifications as the night descends.

> *Pro Tip: Familiarize yourself with the intricacies of "Do Not Disturb" to savor uninterrupted slumber and periods of concentration during critical meetings.*

Privacy and security settings

While notifications emerge as invaluable bearers of information, they concurrently traverse the realm of personal data. It is incumbent upon you to retain a stranglehold on the domains accessible to your applications and to safeguard your privacy with unwavering resolve. **In the inner sanctum of "Settings," steer your course toward the "Privacy" enclave.**

Within this hallowed ground, you are granted the authority to meticulously govern which applications are endowed with access to your location, camera, microphone, contacts, and more. The configuration of these parameters emulates the establishment of boundaries for your digital existence, extending access solely to applications deemed trustworthy.

> *Pro Tip: Recurrently revisit these precincts of privacy settings to perpetually retain dominion over your digital data and to fortify the fortifications protecting your personal information.*

This compendium of indispensable customization and notification management attributes ensures the metamorphosis of your iPhone into an authentic reflection of your predilections and individuality.

With this edifice laid, let us now plunge into the captivating realm of biometric security, a domain governed by the indomitable entities of Face ID and Touch ID.

2.3 Location and Privacy

What are location settings and how to manage them

Your iPhone stands as a potent device reliant on various functionalities, including location services, to amplify your experience. Location settings enable applications to tap into your device's GPS, providing you with pertinent data such as navigation guidance, weather updates, or nearby points of interest. However, striking a delicate balance between utility and safeguarding your privacy remains paramount.

Within your iPhone's "Settings" menu, you'll encounter the "Privacy" section. Here, the management of your device's location settings comes into play. You'll be presented with a roster of applications that have sought access to your location. It's imperative to grant location privileges exclusively to applications that you hold in trust and those that genuinely require this information to fulfill their core functions. For example, granting your mapping app access to your location is logical, whereas a weather app may not necessitate constant tracking.

Pro Tip: Periodically review and refine these settings to uphold a harmonious equilibrium between convenience and privacy.

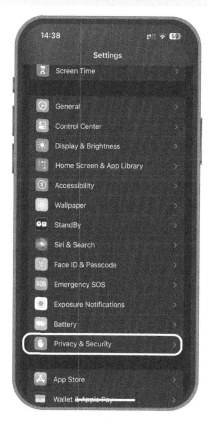

How to ensure privacy for your photos, messages, and other personal data

Your iPhone serves as a repository of personal data, encompassing photographs, messages, sensitive documents, and emails. Safeguarding this data stands as a paramount concern. **Within the "Settings" application, navigate to the "Privacy" section, wherein various categories are presented, including "Photos" and "Messages."** Delving into these categories allows for the regulation of which applications can access your confidential information.

For instance, within the "Photos" section, you can discern which applications have petitioned for entry into your photo library. Scrutinize and administer these permissions with meticulous care. Simultaneously, explore the settings relevant to other data categories, such as "Messages," to ensure the confidentiality of your personal dialogues.

Pro Tip: Regularly revisit these settings to maintain vigilance over the privacy of your data.

Limiting access of specific apps to your data

Certain applications solicit access to your data, encompassing your contacts, photos, or microphone, for sundry purposes. While some applications genuinely necessitate this access for their primary functionality, others may not warrant such privileges. You have the authority to manage these permissions individually, thus maintaining control over your data.

Within the "Privacy" section of your iPhone's settings, seek out "App Permissions." Herein lies a catalog of applications and the categories of data they are capable of accessing. You possess the capability to toggle access on or off for each application, thereby restricting data sharing to solely those applications you hold in confidence.

Pro Tip: Periodically conduct audits of these app permissions to guarantee that solely the applications you are at ease with have access to your data.

By taking charge of your location settings and data permissions, you are not only enhancing your iPhone's privacy but also ensuring its efficacy in serving you. Now, let's delve into the Control Center and its potential to simplify your daily interactions with your iPhone.

2.4 Control Center:
What it is, how to use it, and how to customize it.

Overview of the control center and its quick commands

The Control Center stands as your iPhone's nerve center, easily accessible with a swift downward swipe from the upper-right corner of your screen. **Designed for efficiency, it furnishes rapid access to indispensable functions.** Envision it as your cockpit, where you can toggle **Wi-Fi, Bluetooth**, adjust **brightness**, oversee **music playback**, and execute more with a single tap.

Customizing the Control Center to cater to your unique requirements is an effortless undertaking. **Within the "Settings" menu, under "Control Center," select "Customize Controls."** (See images in the next page.) Here, you possess the liberty to append or omit specific commands. As an illustration, if you engage extensively in note-taking, the inclusion of the **"Notes"** command can economize precious seconds. Conversely, if the **"Apple TV Remote"** feature rarely finds utility in your usage, its omission ensures a streamlined Control Center.

> *Pro Tip: Tailor your Control Center to align with your most frequent tasks, thereby enhancing the efficiency of your iPhone experience.*

Add, remove, and rearrange functions in the control center

Rendering your Control Center distinctly personal hinges on the virtue of customization. To append or eliminate functions, follow the instructions delineated earlier in the "Overview" section. When incorporating functions, deliberate on your daily routine and the actions you most frequently execute on your iPhone. Do you routinely employ the flashlight, calculator, or screen recording?

Adjudicate the composition of your Control Center accordingly to streamline these actions. Recall that you have the latitude to rearrange the sequence of functions within the Control Center, situating your most-favored features prominently. **Simply tap and hold an icon, then manipulate its placement to your preferred location.**

> *Pro Tip: Maintain the organization of your Control Center to expedite access to requisite functions.*

Using brightness and volume control, airplane mode, and do not disturb

The Control Center simplifies the adjustment of your iPhone's settings. A downward swipe unfurls indispensable controls, encompassing screen brightness and volume adjustment. These modifications wield substantial influence over your user experience. As an instance, dimming the screen brightness in low-light scenarios mitigates ocular strain and conserves battery life. The act of modifying volume ensures audibility or hushed serenity as demanded.

Furthermore, **the Control Center extends swift access to airplane mode and "Do Not Disturb."**

Airplane mode proves invaluable during air travel, promptly deactivating the wireless communication functions of your iPhone.

The **"Do Not Disturb"** functionality silences notifications, conferring moments of serenity or dedicated work time.

> *Pro Tip: Proficiency in the functions of the Control Center can render your iPhone experience more fluid and enjoyable by economizing time and effort.*

As you grow adept at wielding the Control Center and tailoring it to your specifications, your iPhone metamorphoses into an extension of your persona, responsive to your requisites with precision.

We shall now embark on the realm of Home Screen customization, affording you the opportunity to arrange and optimize your app layout for maximal efficiency.

2.5 Customize Home Screen

Organizing and grouping apps in folders

Efficiency lies at the core of optimizing your iPhone experience, and this encompasses the meticulous organization of your Home Screen to facilitate seamless access to frequently-used apps. One effective approach entails the creation of folders. To initiate this process, press and hold any app icon until it enters a state of agitation. Subsequently, drag one app atop another, prompting your iPhone to autonomously generate a folder housing both applications.

Assigning descriptive names to these folders, such as "Productivity" or "Games," can significantly augment navigational ease. This nomenclature ensures rapid identification of specific apps, obviating the necessity to sift through an array of icons.

Pro Tip: Periodically scrutinize the organization of your folders to ensure it harmonizes with the evolving patterns of your app utilization.

Adding and removing widgets

Widgets constitute a splendid augmentation to your Home Screen, affording prompt access to information from apps sans the requirement to launch them individually.

A rightward swipe upon your Home Screen unveils the **"Today View,"** your gateway to widgets, which can be further tailored to align with your preferences. By selecting "Edit" at the screen's base, you can seamlessly append or delete widgets.

Customizing widgets confers the ability to tailor your Home Screen, projecting the information of utmost significance to you. Be it forthcoming calendar engagements, meteorological updates, or your preferred news stream, widgets bear the potential to elevate your productivity.

> *Pro Tip: Engage in experimentation with assorted widgets to discern which ones confer the highest value in the context of your day-to-day routine.*

Changing the order of home screen pages

Adapting your iPhone's Home Screen configuration to suit your predilections represents a prudent endeavor. It culminates in heightened accessibility to your apps and widgets. The act of rearranging your Home Screen pages is an uncomplicated process. Execute a press-and-hold gesture upon any app or widget until it initiates a state of agitation. Subsequently, shift it toward the left or right extremity of the screen to translocate it to another page.

Contemplate structuring your Home Screen pages contingent upon the frequency of app utilization. Allocate your most-frequently accessed apps to the initial page, facilitating instantaneous retrieval. By optimizing the layout of your Home Screen, you ameliorate the temporal expenditure entailed in questing for apps, ultimately elevating overall efficiency.

> *Pro Tip: Periodically assess your app usage patterns, enabling the fine-tuning of your Home Screen for the attainment of maximal productivity.*

Additional customization functions and settings for seniors

Apple accords recognition to the diverse demography of its device users, encompassing individuals with varying requirements. **For seniors or users necessitating supplemental assistance, an array of features is accessible under "Settings" > "Accessibility."** These features are tailored to enrich the user experience.

The **"Larger Text"** attribute empowers you to modulate text dimensions across your device, augmenting legibility. **"Magnifier"** effectuates the transformation of your iPhone into a magnifying glass, proficiently employed for perusing fine print or diminutive text. **"VoiceOver"** furnishes auditory feedback, easing navigation for users afflicted with visual impairments.

Pro Tip: Delve into these accessibility attributes to ensure that your iPhone extends user-friendliness, spanning diverse age groups and needs.

The customization of your Home Screen surpasses the realm of aesthetics; it's a strategic approach to streamline your quotidian interactions with your iPhone. As you systematically structure and optimize your Home Screen, you'll discern a surge in the efficiency governing app access and information retrieval. Presently, let us immerse ourselves in the Display and Brightness settings, where the potential to fine-tune your iPhone's visual encounter awaits, promising maximal comfort.

2.6 Display and Brightness

Dark Mode: what it is and how to activate it

Dark Mode represents a display feature engineered to augment legibility and diminish ocular strain, especially when confronted with dim ambient conditions. Enabling Dark Mode can significantly elevate your iPhone interaction. **To set it in motion, proceed to the "Settings" menu, tap "Display & Brightness," and opt for "Dark."**

Pro Tip: To further refine your experience, configure Dark Mode to activate automatically during designated hours or at sundown. This dual benefit not only provides respite to your eyes but also conserves battery life, a double win for users.

True Tone: what it is and how it can help the eyesight

True Tone constitutes another display attribute geared towards enriching your visual experience by harmonizing your screen's white balance with the ambient illumination. This calibration imbues colors with a more natural appearance while diminishing eye fatigue. **Initiating True Tone involves navigating to "Settings," accessing "Display & Brightness," and toggling the "True Tone" switch.**

Pro Tip: For optimal outcomes, it is advisable to leave True Tone enabled since it continuously adapts to diverse lighting scenarios, guaranteeing your iPhone's display consistently delivers impeccable visual quality.

Physical Buttons

Individuals in possession of older iPhone iterations equipped with home buttons can enhance usability by adjusting button settings. **These settings are accessible via the "Settings" menu. First, tap "Accessibility," then select "Touch."** Within this interface, you can fine-tune the click speed and feedback of the home button to align with your preferences.

Pro Tip: Experimentation with these settings is encouraged to ascertain the click speed that exhibits optimal responsiveness to your touch, thereby affording you a smoother navigation experience.

Change the click speed of the home button (for older devices with home button)

The capability to personalize the click speed of your home button holds particular value for owners of older iPhone models. **Within the "Settings" menu, beneath "Accessibility" and "Touch," you can elect between "Default," "Slow," or "Slowest" click velocities.**

Pro Tip: Engage in trials with different click speeds to unearth the one that complements your inclinations. This seemingly minor adjustment can exert a substantial influence on your overall user experience.

Using volume buttons for specific functions, such as taking pictures

The volume buttons adorning the side of your iPhone serve multifarious purposes, including their role as a shutter button within the Camera app. **When operating the Camera app, depression of either the volume up or down button precipitates the capture of a photograph.**

Pro Tip: This feature proves especially advantageous for capturing steady images, particularly in scenarios where tapping the screen may result in unsteady shots. Endeavor to employ the volume buttons to enhance your photographic proficiency.

Text types and display

Customization of your textual experience can exert a transformative effect, particularly if your iPhone engagements entail extensive reading or messaging. **"Settings," "Display & Brightness,"** **contains options such as "Text Size" and "Bold Text."**

Adjust size and style of text

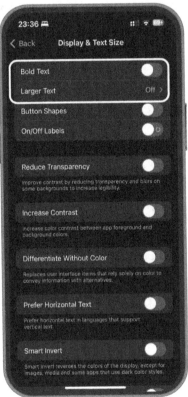

Adjustments to text size and style permit tailoring to your preferences.

Whether your predilection gravitates towards larger, bold text for facile reading or a more minimalist font demeanor, these customization avenues empower finetuning of your iPhone's textual manifestation.

Pro Tip: Dedicate time to experiment with distinct text settings to unearth the ideal textual presentation that accords with your reading comfort.

Spacing lines for easier reading

Customization of the spacing existing between lines of text can exert a pronounced influence on readability. **Within "Settings," traverse to "Accessibility," and designate "Display & Text Size."** In this milieu, you are bestowed with the ability to modify line spacing by activating **"Larger Text" and enabling "Larger Accessibility Sizes."**

> *Pro Tip: Trial a gamut of line spacing configurations until discovery of the one that engenders the most comfortable reading experience for your visual faculties.*

Motion reduction: What it is and how it can help prevent motion sickness or visual vertigo

Motion Reduction represents an invaluable attribute catering to individuals susceptible to motion-induced queasiness or visual unease during iPhone utilization. This characteristic curtails motion effects intrinsic to iOS, consequently ameliorating the comfort and usability of your device.

To activate Motion Reduction, journey to the "Settings" realm, engage "Accessibility," and subsequently elect "Motion." Within this sphere, **engage the "Reduce Motion" toggle.**

  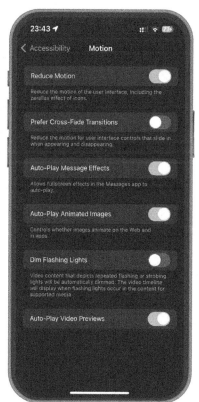

Pro Tip: In scenarios where motion sickness or visual discomfort ensues during iPhone utilization, activating this feature can impart a considerable enhancement in comfort and utility.

Tailoring your iPhone's display and visual settings ensures your device conforms to your distinct predilections and requirements. Whether it involves heightening legibility through Dark Mode, mitigating ocular fatigue with True Tone, or refining text presentation, these configurations contribute to an enriched iPhone experience. The ensuing section delves into keyboard settings and strategies for optimizing your typing proficiency on your iPhone.

2.7 Keyboard

Dictionary Settings and Auto-Correction

The iPhone's keyboard boasts an integrated lexicon that proffers word suggestions and rectifications during text input. This attribute can prove immensely beneficial but occasionally tenders unwarranted suggestions. **To govern these parameters, navigate to "Settings" > "General" > "Keyboard."**

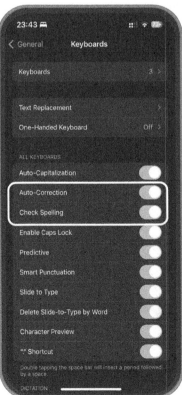

Within this domain, you can activate or deactivate the "Auto-Correction" and "Check Spelling" functions.

By deactivating auto-correction, you assume greater command over your textual entries, especially advantageous for individuals who find auto-correction more vexing than advantageous.

Pro Tip: For those engaged in multilingual text input, dictionaries for different languages can be appended or removed to augment precision, thereby ensuring your iPhone comprehends and honors your diverse linguistic interactions.

Disabling Auto-Correction

The process of deactivating auto-correction is straightforward yet invaluable. Its cessation empowers you to input text unhindered, devoid of predictive or corrective interventions by your iPhone. This proves particularly advantageous when composing content featuring specialized terminology or idiosyncratic language.

To disable auto-correction, adhere to the aforementioned "Keyboard" settings and toggle off "Auto-Correction."

Pro Tip: Disabling auto-correction can be advantageous for writers, professionals, or individuals who prize precision in their textual input. Remember, reactivation remains an option when necessitated.

Set keyboard language preferences

The iPhone is artfully designed to embrace multiple languages, amplifying its versatility as a communication tool. The facile transition between languages can be executed within your keyboard settings.

In the "Keyboards" section, languages can be incorporated or expunged, ensuring that your iPhone adeptly comprehends your multilingual communication imperatives.

Additionally, you can specify your preferred language for dictation and voice input, enabling the articulation of messages and directives in your chosen language.

Pro Tip: For those frequently engaging in multilingual discourse, the activation of multilingual keyboards can save time and effort. This facilitates a seamless shift between languages during text input or voice dictation.

How to install a new keyboard from the App Store

The App Store extends a wide array of third-party keyboards, each poised to elevate your typing proficiency. These keyboards frequently feature distinctive attributes such as swipe typing, gesture controls, or predictive emoji functions.

The installation of a new keyboard from the App Store unfolds as follows:

1. Launch the **App Store** on your iPhone.

2. Execute a search for a keyboard application aligned with your preferences.

3. Download and i**nstall the selected application.**

4. Upon successful installation, access:
"**Settings**" > "**General**" > "**Keyboard**" > "**Keyboards.**"

5. Engage **"Add New Keyboard"** and designate the installed keyboard application.

> *Pro Tip: The realm of third-party keyboards harbors a trove of features tailored to diverse typing styles and requisites. While some keyboards are engineered for speed, others emphasize an extensive repertoire of emojis and stickers to facilitate expressive communication.*

The personalization of keyboard configurations bestows upon you the authority to shape your text input adventure in harmony with your idiosyncratic inclinations and necessities. Whether your quest entails meticulous control over auto-correction, a penchant for multilingual interaction, or a quest to unearth third-party keyboards housing additional functionalities, these settings assure that your iPhone's keyboard conforms to your essence. The ensuing chapter will embark on the domains of automated updates and data preservation—pivotal facets of iPhone preservation and security.

2.8 Automatic Updates

What they are, how to activate or deactivate them

The concept of automated updates stands as a pivotal element in the maintenance of your iPhone's functionality and security. It guarantees that your device's operating system and applications remain current, benefiting from the latest enhancements, bug fixes, and security updates. These updates invariably encompass improvements that enhance your overall user experience.

To manage automatic updates, navigate to **"Settings" > "General" > "Software Update."** Herein, you are presented with two indispensable options: "Download iOS updates" and "Download updates automatically."

> *Pro Tip: Generally, it is prudent to maintain these options in an active state to ensure your iPhone perpetually aligns with the most recent enhancements and security reinforcements. Nevertheless, if you contend with data constraints or harbor a penchant for manual updates, the option to deactivate these features remains at your disposal.*

How to manually keep the iPhone updated

While automatic updates proffer convenience, certain users espouse a more hands-on approach to update installation.

Assuming manual control over your iPhone's update process empowers you to handpick the most opportune moments for these installations, obviating workflow disruptions.

Should an update become available, you will receive a notification.

To instigate a manual update, adhere to the following protocol:

1. Open **"Settings"** on your iPhone.

2. Scroll through the menu and designate **"General."**

3. Subsequently, tap **"Software Update."**

In the event that an update awaits, a prompt will manifest, offering the option to download and install forthwith or schedule the process for a more convenient juncture.

> *Pro Tip: Consistently reviewing updates and effecting prompt installations is imperative to sustain the smooth operation and security of your iPhone. This practice guarantees that you perpetually benefit from cutting-edge features and protection against latent vulnerabilities.*

2.9 Backup and Data Preservation

How to back up on iCloud or a computer

Regularly executing backups for your iPhone stands as an elemental ritual to shield your data against potential loss, damage, or the acquisition of a new device. Apple proffers two primary avenues for effecting iPhone backups: iCloud and computer-based backups. For iCloud backup, undertake the subsequent sequence: **"Settings"** > **[Your Name]** > **"iCloud"** > **"iCloud Backup."**

Within this interface, you can instigate an immediate backup by tapping **"Back Up Now."** Furthermore, activating "iCloud Backup" automates this process. iCloud backups encompass an array of data, including device settings, app data, iMessages, photos, and more.

In the event that you opt for computer-based backups, ensue the ensuing procedure: Affix your iPhone to your computer and open iTunes (or Finder on macOS Catalina and subsequent iterations). Select your device, and subsequently, click "Back Up Now." This ensues in a comprehensive backup of your iPhone to your computer.

> *Pro Tip: It is astute to institute recurring iCloud backups for convenience. Notwithstanding, the curation of periodic backups on your computer is also advised. This dual approach ensures the possession of an additional copy of your data, should exigent circumstances materialize.*

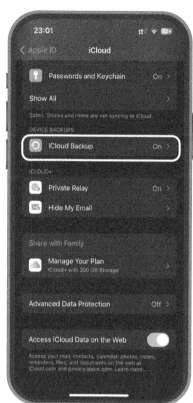

The Importance of Regular Backups

In this era dominated by digital technologies, where iPhones have evolved into reservoirs of cherished memories, vital information, and essential communications, the paramount significance of periodic backups cannot be overstated. **Backups essentially serve as insurance for your invaluable photos, videos, contacts, messages, and application data.** Their importance transcends mere data retrieval convenience; it extends into the realm of emotional solace. The loss of such data, be it a consequence of hardware malfunctions, inadvertent deletions, or device theft, can inflict profound emotional distress. It can equate to a digital history's fragmentary obliteration, and the sentiments associated with these digital relics can be incalculable.

Furthermore, data loss can entail not only emotional tribulations but also operational disruptions in one's daily life. Ponder upon the inconveniences that accompany the loss of your contact roster, vital documents, or the capacity to access indispensable applications.

Regular backups function as a safety harness against such disruptions. They ensure that, in the event of data forfeiture, you can expeditiously reinstate your iPhone to its antecedent state,

curtailing operational downtimes and obviating the necessity for manual data recreation or retrieval endeavors. As our dependency on smartphones deepens, encompassing both personal and occupational facets, the import of ingraining backups as a habitual component of your iPhone maintenance regimen cannot be underscored enough.

> *Pro Tip: To cement the imminence of data safeguarding, consider scheduling reminders for periodic backups. This practice guarantees that even if lapses in memory manifest, your iPhone will prompt you to uphold the sanctity of your data.*

iCloud space: How it works and whether it's worth buying more space

Providing clarity on the mechanics of iCloud storage and methods to monitor and manage your available space is a fundamental objective. Users should garner insights into the diverse tiers of iCloud storage plans, each accompanied by varying storage capacities and correlated costs. These stratified plans encompass the free 5 GB tier and subscription-based alternatives, extending from 50 GB to 2 TB.

Guidance on upgrading one's iCloud storage plan, should recurring space depletion transpire due to photographs, videos, backups, or other data, is imperative. Particular attention should be directed toward the 50 GB plan, which typically caters to the exigencies of most users, particularly when coupled with sporadic manual backups to their computer.

> *Pro Tip: Advocating for users to discern their storage requisites predicated on their usage patterns is paramount. Through comprehension of these exigencies, users can make judicious selections among the array of iCloud storage plans, ensuring alignment with their operational necessities.*

Mastery over automated updates and data preservation methodologies empowers iPhone users to exert influence over their device's operational efficiency, security, and data inviolability. In forthcoming sections, we shall explore advanced features and functionalities, unlocking the full spectrum of potential inherent in iOS 16 devices.

Chapter 3:

Introduction to Accessibility 🎙️

What does accessibility mean?

Accessibility comprises a set of design principles and technologies aimed at guaranteeing the usability of digital content and devices by individuals of varying abilities, encompassing those facing disabilities. In the context of the iPhone, accessibility entails the integration of features that render the device and its functionalities accessible to individuals, regardless of any physical or cognitive constraints they may encounter.

It revolves around cultivating an inclusive milieu where technology serves as a tool for empowerment and self-reliance.

Why is it important for senior users?

Accessibility assumes paramount significance for senior users due to its role in enabling them to fully exploit the capabilities of their iPhones, notwithstanding the age-related alterations that might impact their vision, hearing, motor abilities, and cognitive faculties. By embracing accessibility features, **Apple guarantees that seniors can tailor their devices to cater to their evolving requisites**, thereby fostering sustained connectivity, productivity, and interaction with technology.

3.1 Enhancements for Screen Viewing

In Apple's pursuit of rendering the iPhone more accessible and user-centric, they have introduced a slew of attributes encapsulated under **"Enhancements for Screen Viewing."** These attributes are particularly advantageous for individuals confronting visual impairments or those who simply harbor a penchant for a more finely tailored visual encounter.

Zoom: How to Activate and Use Zoom

Zoom stands as an exceptional accessibility feature, affording users the capability to amplify content displayed on their iPhone's screen. The initiation of Zoom involves a simple sequence: Users should venture into the **"Settings" application, proceed to select "Accessibility," and within the "Vision" segment, make a selection of "Zoom."**

After effecting the actuation of Zoom by **toggling the corresponding switch**, users can seamlessly activate it via the execution of a double-tap on the screen employing three fingers.

Once operational, Zoom facilitates an experience characterized by fluidity and intuitiveness. Users can traverse the magnified view by performing the action of dragging three fingers across the screen. The level of magnification is amenable to adjustment through the straightforward mechanism of executing a double-tap followed by a swiping gesture, utilizing three fingers to incrementally augment or diminish the degree of magnification.

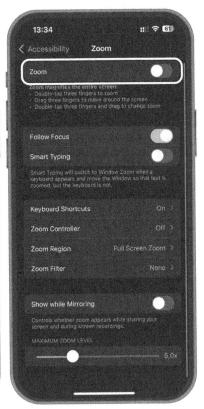

Adjust Settings and Customize the Experience

The premise of customization underpins Apple's accessibility ethos, and Zoom is emblematic of this philosophy. Within the annals of Zoom settings, users are presented with a panoply of options for personalizing their experience.

The Zoom Region provides users with the liberty to elect between options such as "Full Screen Zoom" or "Window Zoom," contingent upon their predilections.

The "Zoom Filter" arena extends choices including "None," "Inverted," or "Grayscale" for the amplification of visibility. Users are further empowered to activate or deactivate the "Follow Focus" function, which proffers the automated magnification of text being entered within a text field, thereby facilitating enhanced visibility during the act of typing. Moreover, Zoom extends the convenience of controller shortcuts, thereby expediting facile access to quintessential zoom functionalities.

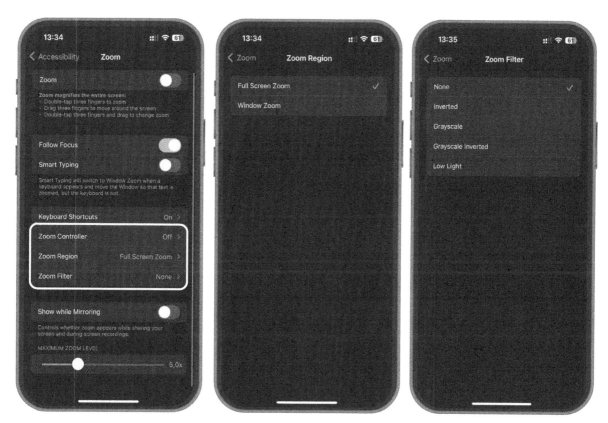

Pro Tip: Dive into the Accessibility settings to explore additional Zoom options, such as the Zoom Filter. Experiment with color schemes like grayscale or inverted colors to enhance readability and reduce eye strain during prolonged screen viewing.

Magnifier: Activation and Usage of the Magnifier

The Magnifier feature, an indispensable component of enhanced screen viewing on the iPhone, is characterized by its ease of initiation and deployment. On your iPhone or iPad, **open the Magnifier app.** If you don't see the Magnifier app, on the Home Screen, swipe down and search for Magnifier.

Magnifier

If you use Magnifier frequently, you can create an Accessibility Shortcut to open it with the triple-click of a button. **You can also add Magnifier to Control Center for easier access. To customize Control Center: Go to Settings > Control Center then tap the Add button next to Magnifier.**

Post-activation, Magnifier is accessed with consummate convenience, necessitating a triple-click of either the side button (for iPhones equipped with Face ID) or the home button (for iPhones endowed with Touch ID). Magnifier epitomizes accessibility through expeditious access and user-friendliness. It harnesses the iPhone's built-in camera to yield a magnified view of objects or text.

The calibration of magnification levels is rendered effortless via the employment of a slider or through the intuitive gesture of pinching the screen. This feature assumes paramount significance in instances involving the perusal of fine print on labels, menus, or any other minuscule text, as well as during meticulous examinations of objects necessitating granular scrutiny.

Customization

Apple is staunch in its commitment to providing users with the ability to personalize their Magnifier experience to harmonize with their unique preferences. **The precincts of Magnifier settings encompass the option to activate or deactivate "Auto-Brightness," a feature designed to augment visibility by modulating lighting conditions.**

Users are further afforded the prerogative to select from an assortment of color filters, thereby bolstering contrast and visibility. Additionally, **users can opt to enable the "Highlight Content" functionality, which accentuates text to enhance its perceptibility.** Through these avenues of customization, individuals grappling with visual impairments can fine-tune Magnifier to cater to their singular requirements.

> *Pro Tip: Optimize the Magnifier's utility by enabling "Auto-Brightness" in the Magnifier settings. This ensures that the magnified view adapts to varying lighting conditions, maintaining clarity and reducing glare.*

Larger Text

How to adjust text size

The **"Larger Text"** accessibility feature is a boon not confined to the purview of visual impairments but extends its beneficence to all users harboring a predilection for more legible text on their iPhones.

The process of configuring Larger Text is a mere trifle. **Users should launch the "Settings" application, delve into "Accessibility," and under the "Display & Text Size" ambit, elect "Larger Text."**

Following the activation of "Larger Accessibility Sizes," a slider materializes, affording users the capacity to calibrate text dimensions in accordance with their predilections.

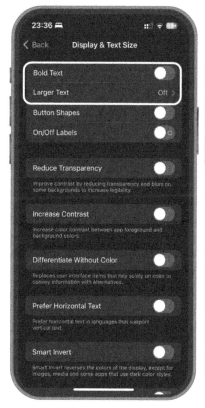 

Setting text in bold

In consonance with the commitment to text lucidity, Apple accords users the means to render text even more readable through the activation of the **"Bold Text" option,** conveniently situated just beneath the text size slider within the precincts of the **"Larger Text" settings.** The enablement of this attribute heightens the prominence of text throughout the iPhone's user interface, engendering a stark clarity that expedites readability.

These enhancements devised for screen viewing, encompassing Zoom, Magnifier, Larger Text, and Bold Text, bequeath unto users the authority to configure their iPhone's display in a manner that conforms to their individual predilections. Whether it entails the magnification of text for effortless perusal, the calibration of text dimensions for augmented legibility, or the amplification of on-screen content clarity, these features are designed to metamorphose the iPhone into an instrument that is both versatile and accessible to one and all.

Pro Tip: Leverage the "Bold Text" option in Display & Text Size settings for a bolder and more distinct text appearance. Adjusting the font weight complements larger text, further enhancing readability.

3.2 High Contrast and Motion Reduction

Apple's dedication to accessibility extends beyond merely enhancing visual elements; it also places emphasis on improving contrast and curbing motion to meet a variety of user requirements.

High Contrast: What It Signifies and How It Can Help

High Contrast mode stands as a robust accessibility feature meticulously crafted to heighten visual clarity, especially catering to users with visual impairments. The activation of High Contrast mode brings forth a substantial augmentation in the contrast ratio between text and background.

This transformation renders text and interface elements far more discernible, offering significant assistance to users who contend with low-contrast interfaces.

Initiating High Contrast mode is an accessible process. **Users can delve into it via the "Settings" application. Within the "Accessibility" section, under the "Display & Text Size" category, an option dubbed "Increase Contrast" can be found.** A mere toggle of this switch activates the High Contrast mode.

Activation and Customization

High Contrast mode is thoughtfully designed to be straightforward and user-friendly. Once engaged, users will promptly discern the augmented contrast pervasive throughout the iPhone's interface.

The background assumes a deeper hue, while text and interface elements adopt a heightened prominence concerning both color and lucidity. This tailored adaptability substantially amplifies the overall user experience, rendering the iPhone a more accessible and user-centric device.

Pro Tip: High Contrast mode is a powerful tool, but you can further tailor it to your preferences. After enabling it, explore the "Accessibility" settings to adjust the contrast to a level that suits your vision best. Experiment with different settings to find the perfect balance between clarity and aesthetics.

Motion Reduction: What It Signifies and How It Can Help

Motion Reduction emerges as a pivotal accessibility feature, particularly suited to individuals who grapple with motion sickness or discomfort while navigating smartphone interfaces. This feature takes deliberate steps to diminish motion effects encompassing parallax motion, animations, and transitions, thereby creating a more seamless and congenial user experience. It emerges as an invaluable addition for users who may find the default animations and transitions disconcerting.

The activation of Motion Reduction is attainable by navigating to the "Settings" application and selecting "Accessibility." Within the purview of the "Motion" section, an option denominated "Reduce Motion" awaits. A mere flick of this switch sets the feature in motion.

Customization

Once set in motion, Motion Reduction warrants no further tailoring. Its effects promptly become discernible as the dynamic motion animations and transitions prevalent within the iPhone's

interface undergo minimization. This culminates in a more static and less visually dynamic user experience, a change that can substantially diminish discomfort for users susceptible to motion-related unease.

> *Pro Tip: Customize the degree of motion reduction in the "Reduce Motion" settings. Tailor the parallax effect to your preference by fine-tuning motion settings in the Accessibility settings.*

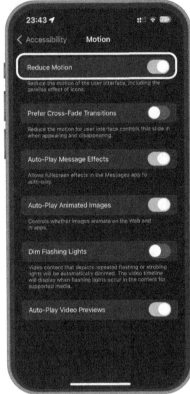

Apple's accessibility features of High Contrast and Motion Reduction are attuned to the distinctive needs of users.

High Contrast augments visual clarity and the legibility of text, rendering the iPhone's interface more accessible.

In contrast, Motion Reduction engineers a smoother user experience through the mitigation of motion effects, ensuring that the iPhone stands as a congenial and user-centric device for individuals who may experience motion-related unease. These features vividly exemplify Apple's unwavering commitment to inclusivity and accessibility.

3.3 Audio Assistance

Apple's unwavering commitment to inclusivity is evident in the spectrum of audio assistance features seamlessly integrated into their iPhones. These features go beyond mere nods to accessibility; they stand as a testament to Apple's dedication to ensuring that every user can harness the complete potential of their device, regardless of their hearing abilities.

In this section, we will delve into these remarkable audio accessibility tools and explore how they empower individuals with varying degrees of hearing impairment to engage with their iPhones in meaningful and enriching ways.

VoiceOver: What it is and how it works

VoiceOver stands as a digital marvel that transforms the iPhone into a formidable tool for individuals with visual impairments. It effectively metamorphoses the device into an auditory interface, meaning that every action, every element on the screen is eloquently described, enabling users to navigate, access apps, read text, and even browse the web without relying on visual cues. VoiceOver is more than just a screen reader; it's a lifeline bridging the gap between the digital realm and users with visual impairments.

The technology underpinning VoiceOver is nothing short of remarkable. When activated, it employs advanced text-to-speech capabilities to audibly articulate the text displayed on the screen. However, its prowess extends beyond mere text rendering. **VoiceOver provides comprehensive audible descriptions of icons, buttons, and other elements, elevating the user experience to a level of richness and immersion that is truly remarkable.**

For instance, when a user taps on an app icon, VoiceOver not only announces the app's name but also guides the user through the available options. Gestures play a pivotal role in interacting with VoiceOver, enabling users to effortlessly perform tasks such as selection, scrolling, and tapping.

Configuration and Use

VoiceOver's distinguishing feature lies in its extensive customizability. Apple acknowledges that accessibility is a highly individualized concept, and users should have the liberty to tailor their experience according to their unique preferences.

Within the VoiceOver settings, users are granted the freedom to fine-tune the experience to match their comfort levels.

Parameters such as speaking rate, voice pitch, and verbosity are all open to adjustment, ensuring that VoiceOver conveys information in a manner that aligns with the user's comfort and familiarity.

Moreover, VoiceOver is accompanied by an exhaustive set of gestures

designed for seamless navigation and interaction. Acquiring proficiency in these gestures is akin to acquiring a new set of skills, opening up a world of possibilities. **Users can explore on-screen elements by swiping left or right, tap once for selection, or employ a two-finger double-tap to activate an item.** These gestures are intuitive and optimized for efficiency, transforming the iPhone into a formidable tool for users with visual impairments.

> *Pro Tip: Explore the VoiceOver rotor settings to configure custom actions. This advanced feature enables personalized navigation shortcuts, streamlining your interactions with apps and content.*

Hearing

In the domain of hearing accessibility, Apple presents an equally impressive array of features and settings aimed at ensuring that everyone, irrespective of their hearing capabilities, can relish crystal-clear audio tailored to their specific requirements.

Made for iPhone Hearing Aids: How to pair and use them

Apple's Made for iPhone (MFi) Hearing Aids epitomize their commitment to inclusivity. These hearing aids are meticulously designed to seamlessly integrate with iPhones, offering users a direct and highly customizable audio experience.

Pairing MFi Hearing Aids with an iPhone is a straightforward process accessible via the "Settings" app. Users can navigate to "Accessibility" and subsequently to "Hearing Devices." Once paired, users gain access to a plethora of features that enable them to optimize their hearing aid experience.

One of the most significant advantages of MFi Hearing Aids is their capacity to synchronize audio directly from the iPhone.

This means that users can stream phone calls, music, and other audio content directly to their hearing aids, bypassing any interference or distortion that may occur when using traditional audio sources.

This direct streaming enhances audio clarity, ensuring that users can engage in conversations and enjoy entertainment to the fullest.

Customize Settings

Hearing needs are as diverse as the individuals themselves, and Apple recognizes this profound diversity. To cater to these variations, Apple offers an array of settings that empower users to customize their audio experience. For instance, users can fine-tune the audio balance between the left and right hearing aids to compensate for any disparities in hearing capabilities. Background noise reduction stands as another invaluable feature, effectively minimizing distractions during conversations or audio playback.

Apple's audio assistance features, particularly VoiceOver and MFi Hearing Aids, are transformative for individuals with visual and hearing impairments. These features transcend the mere realm of accessibility; they are about dismantling barriers and ensuring that every iPhone user can effectively interact with their device, fully enjoying the benefits of modern technology.

The degree of personalization afforded by these features underscores Apple's unwavering commitment to tailoring the user experience to individual needs, rendering iPhones versatile tools capable of accommodating individuals with diverse accessibility requirements. These features not only empower users; they also epitomize Apple's ethos of inclusivity and its dedication to shaping a more accessible and equitable digital world.

> *Pro Tip: Opt for real-time audio sharing with compatible hearing aids, allowing you to share audio from videos or music with a friend who also has Made for iPhone hearing aids. This feature enhances the shared listening experience.*

3.4 Subtitles and Captions

Subtitles and captions stand as indispensable accessibility features that profoundly enhance the iPhone experience for users who are deaf or hard of hearing. These features also benefit those who prefer to consume multimedia content in noisy environments or situations where audio is impractical.

By offering textual representations of spoken dialogue and sounds, subtitles and captions ensure that individuals can seamlessly access and comprehend content. In this comprehensive exploration, we will delve into the activation and customization of these features, their compatibility with diverse apps and multimedia content, and the substantial impact they have on fostering content accessibility and inclusivity.

Activation and Customization

Activating subtitles and captions on your iPhone is an uncomplicated process, guaranteeing real-time access to textual representations of audio content. To enable these features and tailor them to your preferences, adhere to these steps:

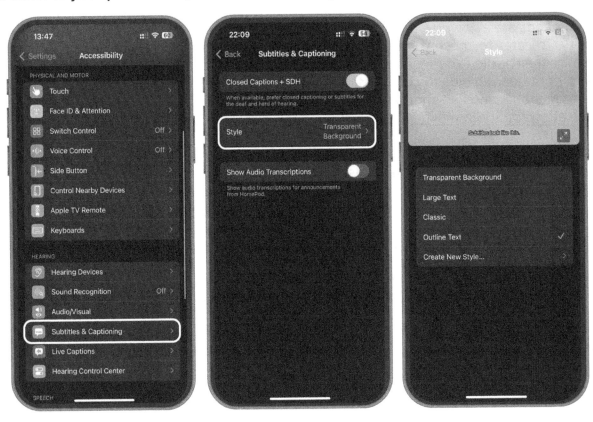

1. **Open "Settings"**: Commence by tapping the **"Settings"** app on your iPhone's home screen. This serves as the hub for configuring various device settings, including accessibility features.

2. **Accessibility Settings**: Traverse the settings menu until you locate and select **"Accessibility"** within the available options. This section hosts a wide array of accessibility features designed to enhance the user-friendliness and inclusivity of the iPhone.

3. **Subtitles & Captioning**: Within the Accessibility menu, **"Subtitles & Captioning"** awaits your selection. Tapping on this option grants access to the settings governing these features.

4. **Toggle On**: On the Subtitles & Captioning screen, activate the **"Closed Captions + SDH"** option by toggling it to the "on" position. This action ensures the display of subtitles and captions when supported by the content.

5. **Customization**: To align subtitles and captions with your preferences, tap on **"Style"** under **"Closed Captions + SDH."** Here, you wield the freedom to adjust numerous visual elements, including text size, font style, text color, and background color. These customizations ensure that subtitles and captions are not only legible but also tailored to your viewing comfort, seamlessly integrated into your content experience.

By enabling and customizing subtitles and captions on your iPhone, you foster a more inclusive and accessible multimedia experience, whether you engage with movies, videos, or other forms of content.

Use with Apps and Multimedia Content

A remarkable facet of subtitles and captions on the iPhone is their compatibility with a plethora of apps and multimedia content. Apple has seamlessly woven these features into its ecosystem, ensuring that users can relish accessible content across diverse applications and services.

Video and Streaming Apps:

Leading video streaming services and apps, including **Netflix**, **Amazon Prime Video**, and **Apple TV**, are champions of subtitles and captions. **These platforms grant users the ability to activate subtitles or captions within the app's settings while enjoying video content.**

For instance, **on Netflix, users can tap the screen during playback, select "Audio & Subtitles,"** and choose their preferred language or subtitle style.

YouTube:

YouTube, a global video behemoth, extends robust support for subtitles. Users can find subtitles in multiple languages for a vast array of videos. **To enable subtitles on YouTube, a simple tap of the "CC" button within the video player suffices.** Furthermore, YouTube offers automatic captions generated by advanced machine learning algorithms, expanding content accessibility to a broader audience.

YouTube

Apple TV and iTunes:

Apple's proprietary streaming service, Apple TV+, along with **content acquired through iTunes, boasts comprehensive support for subtitles and captions.** Users can seamlessly adjust the appearance of subtitles and captions to ensure optimal readability, aligning with their personal preferences.

Accessibility Shortcut:

Apple has thoughtfully incorporated an accessibility shortcut feature, providing swift access to subtitle and caption settings. **To activate this feature, navigate to "Settings" > "Accessibility" > "Accessibility Shortcut," and opt for "Subtitles & Captioning."**

Subsequently, by triple-pressing the side button (on iPhone X and later) or the home button (on earlier iPhone models), users can swiftly toggle subtitles and captions on and off, elevating convenience and accessibility.

The Profound Impact of Subtitles and Captions

In essence, subtitles and captions transcend the realm of mere auxiliary features; they are indispensable accessibility tools that render multimedia content more inclusive and accessible to an extensive audience. They are instrumental in democratizing information and entertainment, dismantling language barriers, and ensuring that everyone, regardless of their hearing capabilities or

linguistic preferences, can engage with and comprehend content. These features are particularly indispensable for individuals who are deaf or hard of hearing, serving as a vital lifeline to the auditory world. Subtitles and captions also extend their benevolence to those who may miss spoken words due to environmental noise or other distractions. Furthermore, they augment comprehension for language learners, enabling them to follow along with spoken dialogue.

Subtitles and captions are more than mere language translation; they grant access to sound effects, speaker identification, and the emotional nuances conveyed through tone of voice. This depth of information guarantees a richer, more immersive experience for all users.

Beyond their direct benefits for accessibility, subtitles and captions play a pivotal role in fostering a more inclusive and diverse media landscape. Content creators are increasingly recognizing the importance of captioning their videos, ensuring that they are accessible to a global audience. In doing so, they not only broaden their viewership but also exemplify their commitment to inclusivity.

Subtitles and captions on the iPhone are not mere technological features; they are tools that empower individuals to access information and entertainment on their own terms. They epitomize the principles of inclusivity and equitable access, ensuring that everyone, regardless of their hearing abilities, language proficiencies, or environmental constraints, can partake in the captivating world of multimedia content. By comprehending how to activate, personalize, and harness these features effectively, iPhone users actively contribute to a more inclusive and accessible digital landscape that benefits all.

> *Pro Tip: Investigate third-party apps that offer extensive subtitle customization options. Some apps provide advanced features like adjustable subtitle delay and multiple language support.*

3.5 Flash LED Blinking Notifications

Flash LED Blinking Notifications stand as a pivotal accessibility feature on the iPhone, meticulously crafted to ensure users remain attuned to crucial alerts, even when enveloped in environments where sound lies dormant or beyond audible reach.

This ingenious feature capitalizes on the iPhone's rear LED flash, typically associated with the device's camera, ingeniously repurposing it to furnish a visual harbinger of incoming notifications—be they calls, messages, emails, or app-related prompts. In this segment, we shall delve into the process of enabling Flash LED Blinking Notifications and expound upon scenarios wherein their worth is most evident.

How to Activate Flash LED Blinking Notifications

The activation of Flash LED Blinking Notifications on your iPhone transpires with consummate ease. Here is an illustrative guide delineating the steps to unleash this feature:

1. **Open "Settings"**: Initiate the process by a gentle tap upon the **"Settings" application** adorning your iPhone's home screen. This bastion houses a spectrum of configuration options, inclusive of those pertaining to accessibility features.

2. **Proceed to Accessibility Settings**: Navigating the labyrinthine realms of the settings menu, direct your selection to **"Accessibility"** from the expansive pantheon of choices presented. Within this precinct, a diverse array of accessibility features awaits, all designed to endow the iPhone with user-friendliness and inclusivity.

3. **Audio/Visual**: Amidst the labyrinthine Accessibility menu, your quest leads you to the hallowed halls of **"Audio/Visual."** It is within these precincts that settings that orchestrate the synergy between the auditory and visual facets of accessibility reside.

4. **LED Flash for Alerts**: Under the banner of **"Audio/Visual,"** the sanctuary you seek bears the name **"LED Flash for Alerts."** By enkindling this feature, marked by the shift of a toggle **switch to the "on" position**, you galvanize your iPhone's LED flash to pulsate upon the arrival of notifications.

With Flash LED Blinking Notifications unfurled and aglow, your iPhone becomes a stage for the visual ballet of a blinking LED flash each time notifications grace your digital realm.

This feature stands as an unwavering sentinel, ensuring that you remain promptly apprised of important messages, calls, or alerts, even when your device's auditory faculties repose in silence or retreat beyond the bounds of audibility.

When Flash LED Blinking Notifications Are Useful

Flash LED Blinking Notifications ascend to prominence, demonstrating their mettle across a kaleidoscope of scenarios:

1. **Muted Sound**: In moments when your iPhone assumes the mantle of silence through modes such as "Do Not Disturb" or silent configurations, auditory notifications slumber. Flash LED Blinking Notifications emerge as vigilant sentinels, beaming forth visual alerts to thwart the inadvertent neglect of critical notifications, particularly within tranquil or formal settings.

2. **Noisy environments**: Amidst the tumult and dissonance of cacophonous milieus where auditory notification sounds are entombed beneath layers of clamor—picture the thronging café or bustling thoroughfare—the luminous cadence of the LED flash unfailingly delivers a conspicuous visual alert.

3. **Hearing Imparements**: For individuals grappling with hearing impairments or navigating the realm of deafness, Flash LED Blinking Notifications assume the mantle of indispensability. They erect a bridge between sound-dependent notifications and the auditory straits of these users, furnishing a seamless flow of information.

4. **Accessibility and Inclusivity**: This feature embodies the spirit of accessibility and inclusivity that courses through the iPhone's digital veins, harmonizing with Apple's unwavering commitment to providing technology that extends its embrace to a kaleidoscope of users.

5. **Privacy**: When circumstances beckon you to ensconce your device in silence, either as an emblem of courtesy within venues such as theaters or during the hushed precincts of pivotal meetings, Flash LED Blinking Notifications surface as the epitome of discretion—a mode to receive notifications that leaves tranquility untouched.

Flash LED Blinking Notifications constitute a pivotal accessibility feature, elevating the iPhone's functionality for a diverse spectrum of users. Through the alchemy of providing a visual cue for incoming notifications, this feature unfailingly ensures that users remain cognizant, irrespective

of their auditory abilities or the circumambient environs. The simple act of activating this feature represents a profound gesture in rendering your iPhone more inclusive and adaptable to the manifold facets of life's diverse tapestry.

> *Pro Tip: Utilize automation apps to create intricate LED notification patterns. You can set up conditional triggers that activate specific LED patterns based on various factors, such as time of day or location.*

3.6 Assistive Touch

The existence of Assistive Touch stands as a testament to Apple's unwavering commitment to fostering inclusivity and accessibility within the iPhone ecosystem. It serves as a versatile and user-centric solution, meticulously designed for individuals who may encounter impediments when engaging with touchscreens or physical buttons.

In this all-encompassing exploration, we shall delve deeply into the multifaceted world of Assistive Touch: its offerings, adept usage, and the enthralling realm of crafting and customizing gestures. This allows users to tailor their iPhone experience to align harmoniously with their specific requisites and predilections.

What assistive touch offers and how to use it

Fundamentally, Assistive Touch manifests as a virtual on-screen menu, serving as an entry point to an array of functionalities and gestures typically executed via physical buttons or complex multi-finger touchscreen maneuvers. Initiating Assistive Touch is a straightforward endeavor.

Abide by these lucid steps for its activation:

> Begin by unearthing the **"Settings" app** within your iPhone.
>
> Scroll the menu's expanse and locate **"Accessibility."**
>
> Under the **"Touch" settings**, you will find **"AssistiveTouch"**. Select it
>
> Toggle the **switch to enable Assistive Touch.**

Upon activation, a diminutive, semi-translucent on-screen button will appear, becoming your conduit to a multitude of functionalities. This button serves as the gateway to an enriched user experience, rendering the iPhone more accessible to a diverse range of users.

- **Home**: This function serves as a surrogate for the physical home button, ushering users back to the home screen with a singular tap.

- **Device**: Here, one can access pivotal device actions, including screen locking, volume adjustments, screenshot captures, and even the emulation of a shake gesture.

- **Control Center**: This option grants a ticket to the Control Center's shortcuts, simplifying tasks such as regulating screen brightness, altering volume levels, and overseeing music playback.

- **Notifications**: The gateway to the notification center swings wide open, streamlining the process of perusing and managing incoming notifications.

- **Custom**: Assistive Touch empowers users to orchestrate bespoke actions and gestures, tailored to their idiosyncratic requirements, a realm we shall explore in greater detail shortly.

- **Siri**: This button ushers forth Siri, Apple's voice-activated digital assistant, providing an alternative mode of interaction with the iPhone.

Assistive Touch substantially enhances the iPhone's accessibility quotient, especially for individuals who may grapple with intricate multi-touch gestures or contend with the challenges posed by physical buttons due to mobility limitations, manual dexterity constraints, or other impediments. Furthermore, it extols the longevity of physical buttons by mitigating their wear and tear, contributing to the device's durability.

Creating and Customizing Gestures

Amongst the most remarkable facets of Assistive Touch resides the ability to conjure and tailor gestures according to one's needs. This feature endows users with the power to conceive and enact specific touchscreen actions with consummate ease, transforming Assistive Touch into a versatile tool for personalization and efficiency.

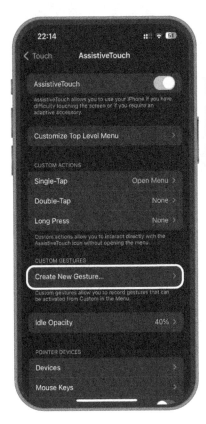  

For the creation of a customized gesture, follow these procedural guidelines:

Open the **Assistive Touch menu** by invoking the on-screen button.

Select **"Custom"** from the menu offerings.

Choose **"Create New Gesture" option**.

On the gesture creation screen, **use your finger to trace the desired gesture across the screen.** As you traverse this digital terrain, a visual representation of your gestural handiwork unfurls.

Once you are satisfied with the rendered gesture, **tap "Save,"** situated in the uppermost right corner.

Give your custom gesture a name and tap "Save."

The resultant custom gesture now stands poised for deployment. Assign it to specific actions or functions within the Assistive Touch menu. This capability is profoundly versatile, affording you the opportunity to design gestures that emulate common multi-touch actions, replicate swipes, pinches, or taps, and even orchestrate intricate concatenations of actions through a solitary gestural enactment. For instance, one could fashion a custom gesture that mimics a three-finger swipe downward, facilitating access to the Control Center, or a double-tap gesture that serves as the clarion call for Siri's emergence. The realm of possibilities stretches boundlessly, constrained solely by the tapestry of your creativity and the particularities of your requirements.

Assistive Touch stands as a testament to Apple's allegiance to accessibility and personalization within the realm of iOS. It unfurls as an elegant solution for users who may confront challenges when navigating conventional touchscreen gestures or engaging physical buttons. By furnishing swift entry to pivotal functions and the capacity to craft custom gestures, Assistive Touch metamorphoses the iPhone into a device marked by versatility and adaptability, epitomizing Apple's steadfast devotion to extending the hand of technology to encompass every individual, regardless of their unique circumstances or abilities.

Pro Tip: Harness the power of Apple's Shortcuts app to create complex automation workflows triggered by Assistive Touch gestures. This enables you to perform sequences of actions with a single tap.

3.7 Touch Response and Waiting Time

In a world where technology plays an ever-expanding role in our daily lives, the concept of personalization has ascended to paramount importance. Each individual possesses a unique array of preferences and needs, and technology that can adapt to these differences undeniably enriches the user experience. Apple, a trailblazer in the tech industry, has astutely recognized the significance of personalization, and the Touch Response and Waiting Time settings, nestled within the Accessibility menu of iPhones, vividly exemplify this unwavering commitment.

In this in-depth exploration, we shall embark on a journey through these settings, unveiling the profound extent of customization they offer and the transformative potential they hold for altering the way you interact with your iPhone.

Adjusting Touch Sensitivity: Your iPhone, Your Rules

Have you ever yearned for your iPhone to better comprehend your touch preferences? It's conceivable that you've encountered inadvertent taps or perceived your touchscreen as occasionally unresponsive. The Touch Sensitivity setting is the solution to these dilemmas, allowing users to finely calibrate the responsiveness of their iPhone's touchscreen. This ensures that the touchscreen aligns precisely with their distinctive touch preferences.

To embark on this journey of customization, follow these steps:

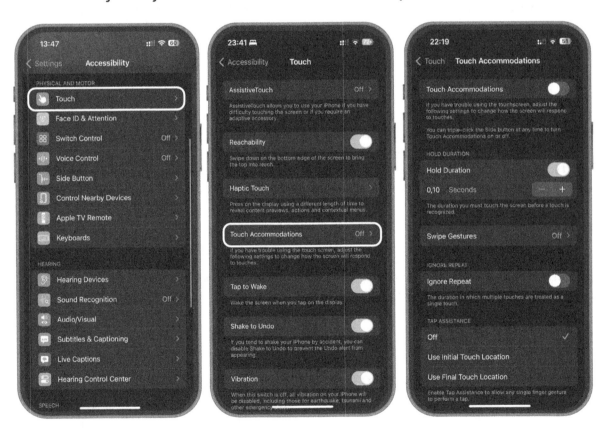

Begin by unlocking your iPhone and navigating the **"Settings" app**, your portal to an expansive realm of customization and accessibility.

Scroll downwards until you alight upon the **"Accessibility"** menu, an enclave brimming with features designed to augment your iPhone experience, fostering inclusivity.

Within the hallowed halls of **"Accessibility,"** journey into the **"Touch" section** – a domain where touch preferences metamorphose into reality.

Among the myriad touch-related options, the **"Touch Accomodations"** setting stands as your gateway to customizing your iPhone's touch response.

Turn on **"Touch Accomodations"**.

To fully apprehend the impacts of your adjustments, engage with your iPhone's touchscreen. Delve into experimentation with various sensitivity levels until you unearth the precise balance that resonates with your tactile inclinations.

The Touch Sensitivity setting introduces an entirely new facet of control into your iPhone experience, curbing the likelihood of inadvertent taps or frustrated inputs. Its merits shine particularly bright for individuals grappling with fine motor control challenges or those inclined toward a less reactive touch experience. Such a level of customization vividly embodies Apple's commitment to tailoring the iPhone to harmonize with the distinct requisites and inclinations of each user.

Setting Waiting Time Between Touches: Empowering Precision

For individuals contending with tremors, unsteady hands, or motor control impediments, unintentional multiple touch inputs can be a wellspring of exasperation. This is precisely where the Waiting Time Between Touches setting emerges as a beacon of hope, endowing users with the ability to delineate the temporal interval requisite for their iPhone to acknowledge a subsequent touch input.

To harness the power of this feature, follow these directives:

Start by opening the **"Settings" app** on your iPhone, the conduit to a universe of customization and accessibility.

Scroll down through the menu's layers until you stumble upon the **"Accessibility"** menu – a veritable sanctuary of features engineered to metamorphose your iPhone into an extension of your unique self.

Within the **"Accessibility"** menu, exploring the **"Touch" section,** the gateway to a meticulously tailored touchscreen experience.

Among the touch-related options, you will find **"Haptic Touch"** – the dwelling of the "Touch Duration" setting, where your touchscreen odyssey continues.

Choose the Touch duration, three predetermined durations – **"Default," "Fast,"** and **"Slow"** – unfurl before your eyes.

Each duration embodies a distinct waiting time between touches, with **"Default"** harboring the swiftest delay and **"Slow"** harboring the most protracted interlude.

Select the duration that seamlessly resonates with your unique requirements and preferences.

The Waiting Time Between Touches setting stands as a potent tool, empowering users to ensure that their touchscreen interactions transpire with surgical precision. No longer must you grapple with the specter of inadvertent gestures usurping your user experience. Through the act of personalizing the waiting time, your iPhone solemnly pledges that multi-touch actions transpire with intentionality, devoid of unintended inputs.

The Touch Response and Waiting Time settings ascend beyond the realm of mere options nestled within your iPhone's accessibility menu. They embody the quintessence of Apple's unwavering allegiance to inclusivity, acknowledging that every user's touch journey is unique.

These settings endow individuals with a diverse array of needs and inclinations, rendering the iPhone an accessible and adaptive tool for all. Whether you yearn for a softer touch or deliberate multi-touch actions, these settings ensure that your iPhone responds precisely as you envision, catapulting your overarching iPhone experience to unprecedented echelons of personalization and inclusivity.

> *Pro Tip: Employ gesture customization to assign multifunctional gestures. These gestures can execute different actions based on the number of taps or the direction of swipes, optimizing your touch experience.*

3.8 Siri and Dictation: Voice Commands with Siri

In the vast realm of technology, where convenience reigns supreme, Apple has always been a pioneer, consistently pushing the boundaries to make interactions with your devices more natural and intuitive. Enter Siri and Dictation, two treasures within the iOS ecosystem that have transformed the way we interact with our iPhones. In this thorough exploration of voice commands and hands-free text input, we'll embark on a journey to uncover the depths of these features, revealing their complexities, and showcasing their incredible potential.

Configuration and usage tips

Siri, your dependable virtual assistant, is like having a personal helper ready at your service. To make the most of Siri, it's important to set it up according to your preferences and understand the many ways it can simplify your digital life. Here's a breakdown of how to get the most out of Siri:

Enabling Siri:

First, make sure Siri is turned on for your device. **Go to "Settings," scroll down to "Siri & Search," and switch on "Listen for 'Hey Siri'."** This feature allows Siri to respond to your voice commands even when your iPhone is in sleep mode.

Customizing Your Experience:

Siri is designed to be flexible and adaptable. **You can tweak its behavior to suit your preferences.**

In the same "Siri & Search" settings, explore options such as "Language," "Voice Feedback," and "My Information" to tailor Siri's responses and improve its understanding of your commands.

Activating Siri:

Starting a conversation with Siri is as simple as saying **"Hey Siri"** followed by your request or holding down the side button (or home button on older devices). Try both methods to discover which one works best for you.

Voice Commands:

Siri's capabilities are vast and always expanding. You can use it to send messages, make calls, set reminders, play music, get directions, and even control your smart home devices. **For instance, saying "Hey Siri, send a message to John" opens a path to composing and sending a message without touching your device.**

Personalizing Your Virtual Assistant:

Siri's voice doesn't have to be boring; it can match your personality and preferences. You can choose from various accents and languages to make your interactions with Siri more enjoyable and relatable.

Exploring Siri Shortcuts:

One of Siri's most amazing features is Siri Shortcuts. This feature lets you create personalized, automated tasks triggered by specific phrases. For example, you can create a custom shortcut like "I'm going home" that sends a text to your family, adjusts your thermostat, and provides navigation instructions—all with a single voice command.

Being Creative:

Don't limit Siri to just everyday tasks. Ask it questions, seek trivia, or even engage in light-hearted banter. Siri's responses often come with a touch of humor and personality.

Privacy Reminder:

While Siri is incredibly helpful, remember that your interactions are recorded and analyzed to improve Siri's accuracy and effectiveness. You can review and delete your Siri history in **"Settings"> "Siri & Search" > "Siri & Dictation History."**

In the realm of voice assistants, Siri truly stands out with its extensive functionality, linguistic flexibility, and adaptability to your unique preferences. By setting up Siri to match your usage patterns, you unlock a world of hands-free convenience that can transform the way you interact with your iPhone.

Creating custom shortcuts

Siri Shortcuts, an essential part of Siri's ecosystem, gives you the power to design your own digital interactions. These customizable commands enable you to create sequences of actions that Siri can perform with a single phrase. Think of it as having your personal digital assistant that follows your every command.

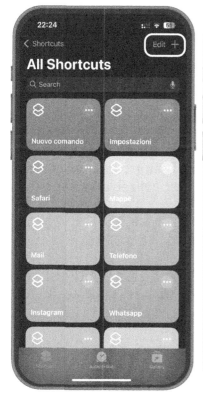

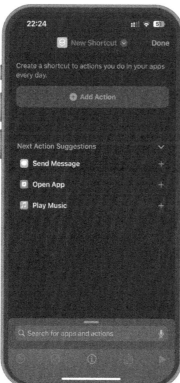

Creating a Siri Shortcut:

To start building your Siri Shortcut collection, open the **"Shortcuts" app** on your iPhone. Tap the **"+" icon to create a new shortcut.** From here, you have various actions at your disposal. You can combine these actions creatively to simplify your digital life.

Personal Phrases:

Once you've put together the perfect sequence of actions for your shortcut, give it a unique phrase that Siri will recognize. For instance, you can make a shortcut called "I'm home" that turns on your lights, adjusts your thermostat, and plays your favorite playlist with a simple phrase.

Suggested Shortcuts:

Shortcuts

If you're not sure where to start, check out the **"Gallery" within the Shortcuts app**. Here, you'll discover a selection of pre-made shortcuts for inspiration. These shortcuts cover a range of scenarios, from making you more productive to adding some fun and quirky commands.

Integration with Apps:

Siri Shortcuts are highly versatile and can integrate with third-party apps. If you have a favorite app that supports Siri Shortcuts, you can automate tasks within that app too. For example, a fitness app could offer shortcuts for tracking workouts or logging meals.

Location-Based Shortcuts:

Siri Shortcuts can also activate based on your location. This means you can set up a shortcut that automatically sends a text to your family when you arrive home or starts your favorite podcast as soon as you get into your car.

Streamlining Routines:

Think about your daily routines and repetitive tasks. Are there actions you do regularly that could be simplified with a Siri Shortcut? Whether it's sending a "Good morning" message to a loved one or ordering your favorite coffee with a voice command, Siri Shortcuts can make your life more efficient.

Accessibility and Inclusivity:

Siri Shortcuts also make technology more accessible and inclusive. They can greatly help individuals with disabilities by reducing the steps needed to perform specific tasks. Siri Shortcuts are a testament to Apple's dedication to user-friendly design and the desire to make technology work for you, not the other way around. By diving into the world of shortcuts and creating commands tailored to your needs, you turn your iPhone into a highly personalized and responsive digital companion.

Dictation

Imagine being able to convert your thoughts, messages, and notes into text using just your voice. Dictation, a feature closely related to Siri, lets you do precisely that. It's a powerful tool that can be your secret weapon for efficient and accurate text input.

Accessing Dictation:

Dictation is conveniently available in almost any situation where you need to type text.

To activate it:

> **Open an app or field where text input is required.** This could be Messages, Notes, Safari, or any other text-based app.

> Tap the **on-screen keyboard** to bring it up.

> Locate the **microphone icon,** usually next to the space bar.

> **Tap the microphone icon** to start using dictation.

Voice to Text:

Once dictation is activated, it's time to let your voice do the talking.
Speak clearly and naturally, and your words will be transcribed into text in real-time. Dictation works remarkably well, thanks to advanced voice recognition technology.

Punctuation and Formatting:

Dictation isn't just about plain text. You can dictate punctuation and formatting instructions to add structure and clarity to your text. For instance, you can say "comma," "period," or "new paragraph" to insert these elements seamlessly.

Support for Multiple Languages:

Dictation is available in several languages, making it a valuable tool for users worldwide. You can dictate in your preferred language, and the system will accurately transcribe your words.

Editing and Corrections:

Dictation is highly accurate, but occasional errors may occur. If you notice a mistake in your transcribed text, you can manually edit it by tapping on the text and making necessary corrections. This flexibility ensures your final text is just as you want it.

Contextual Awareness:

Dictation is aware of context, which means it can adapt to different situations. For example, if you're composing an email, you can say "new paragraph" or "new line" to structure your message properly. During a web search, you can ask a question, and Dictation will understand your intent.

Offline and Privacy:

Dictation works both online and offline, depending on your internet connection. It respects your privacy because the processing of your voice input happens on your device, not in the cloud.

Boosting Productivity:

Dictation is a productivity enhancer, especially when typing can be slow or inconvenient. You can dictate long emails, take notes during meetings, jot down ideas on the fly, or even create entire documents without touching your device.

Accessibility and Inclusion:

Dictation is a game-changer for people with disabilities that may affect traditional typing. It levels the playing field, allowing everyone to engage with technology effortlessly.

Practice for Improvement:

Like any skill, dictation becomes more effective with practice. The more you use it, the better the system adapts to your voice and speech patterns, resulting in increasingly accurate transcriptions.

Privacy and Security:

It's essential to remember that while Dictation offers convenience, your voice input is sent to Apple's servers for processing. However, Apple has strict privacy measures in place to safeguard your data, and you can review and delete your Siri and Dictation history in your device's settings.

In a world where time is precious, and multitasking is the norm, dictation emerges as a valuable tool for efficient and hands-free text input. Whether you're a busy professional, a student taking notes, or simply looking to streamline your messaging, dictation can become your preferred method for text input, boosting your productivity and accessibility in the digital world.

Siri and Dictation: A Dynamic Combination for Enhanced Efficiency

Siri and Dictation are not isolated features but a dynamic duo that can redefine your interactions with your iPhone. By harnessing the power of voice commands and hands-free text input, you unlock new levels of efficiency, accessibility, and personalization.

Imagine starting your day with "Hey Siri, good morning," and having your virtual assistant greet you, summarize your appointments, read your emails aloud, and provide traffic updates for your commute. Later, during a meeting, you effortlessly take notes using Dictation, leaving your hands free for more engagement. At home, you say, "Siri, it's movie night," and your virtual assistant dims the lights, starts your favorite movie, and orders your preferred takeout.

The synergy between Siri and Dictation goes beyond convenience; it's about giving you control over your digital world. The ability to create custom shortcuts tailored to your specific needs, combined with the precision of hands-free text input, transforms your iPhone into a versatile and adaptable tool.

To make the most of Siri and Dictation, keep exploring their capabilities, experiment with custom commands, and fine-tune their settings to match your preferences. Embrace their accessibility features and see how they enhance the lives of individuals with disabilities, making technology more inclusive.

In this rapidly changing digital landscape, **Siri and Dictation are your allies, simplifying the complex, reducing friction in your daily tasks, and ultimately empowering you to get the most out of your iPhone.** By mastering these features, you pave the way for a more efficient, accessible, and personalized digital future.

Pro Tip: Create Siri Shortcuts that integrate with third-party apps, extending Siri's capabilities beyond native functions. This allows you to perform intricate tasks with voice commands, enhancing productivity.

Chapter 4:

Calls, iMessage, and SMS 🎤

Effective communication forms the core of every smartphone, and your iPhone offers a treasure trove of features to help you stay connected. In this chapter, we will delve into the fundamental functions of placing and receiving calls, along with some useful features that enhance your calling experience.

4.1 Essential Functions: Initiating and Accepting Calls

At its essence, a smartphone serves as a communication tool, and the iPhone excels in this realm. Here, we'll explore the essential actions of making and receiving calls, along with some convenient features that enrich your calling experience.

Answering a Call:

When an incoming call arrives, the caller's name or number will appear on your screen. **To accept the call, swipe right on the screen, or press the side button** (or the top button on older models) **once**. If your iPhone is locked, a single press of the side button (or top button) will also answer the call.

Declining a Call:

If you wish **to decline a call, simply tap the red "Decline" button when it appears on the screen.** Alternatively, you can press the side button (or top button) twice to send the call to voicemail.

Making a Call:

Placing a call on your iPhone is a straightforward process. **Launch the "Phone" app, located on your home screen, and tap the keypad icon at the bottom.**

Then, utilize the keypad to **input the number you intend to call, and press the green "Call" button.**

Alternatively, **you can tap a contact in your address book** and subsequently tap their phone number to initiate a call.

> *Pro Tip: Create custom call handling rules using the Shortcuts app to automate responses based on specific criteria, such as caller ID or time of day. This advanced automation enhances call management.*

Using the Address Book:

Effective contact management is pivotal. The "Contacts" app on your iPhone serves as your digital address book.

You can add new contacts by tapping the "+" icon in the upper-right corner and entering their information.

For editing an existing contact, simply open it and tap **"Edit"** in the upper-right corner. You can search for contacts by scrolling through your list or employing the search bar at the top of the Contacts app.

Customizing Ringtones:

Infuse your iPhone with your personality by assigning unique ringtones to specific contacts. This way, you can identify callers without even glancing at your phone.

To set a custom ringtone for a contact, open the "Contacts" app, select the contact, tap "Edit," and then scroll down to the "Ringtone" section. Pick the ringtone of your choice, and it will play when that contact calls you.

Using Speakerphone and Headphones:

The iPhone offers diverse methods for conducting phone calls. **To switch to speakerphone during a call, tap the "Speaker" icon on the call screen.** This proves useful when you want a hands-free conversation or wish to involve others. If you seek enhanced privacy or superior audio quality, consider using headphones or Bluetooth earbuds. Connect them to your iPhone before or during a call and select the desired audio output device in the call screen options.

Blocking Unwanted Numbers:

Unwanted calls and spam are regrettable aspects of modern communication. Luckily, your iPhone equips you with tools to block such numbers.

To block a number, access the "Phone" app, proceed to the "Recents" tab, locate the unwanted call, tap the "i" icon adjacent to it, and scroll down to select "Block this Caller." Moreover, you can block calls and texts from specific contacts in the "Settings" app under "Phone" or "Messages."

> *Pro Tip: Employ machine learning-based call screening apps that continuously update their spam databases to stay ahead of unwanted calls. These apps offer advanced call blocking and filtering options.*

By mastering these fundamental calling functions and contact management, you'll be well-prepared to handle phone calls proficiently and maintain connections with your contacts. In the ensuing sections, we'll delve into advanced features such as iMessage, SMS, multimedia sharing, and privacy settings to elevate your communication experience with your iPhone.

4.2 iMessage, emojis, and groups

Let's dive into the colorful realm of iMessage, the messaging platform that takes your conversations beyond plain text messages. From understanding what makes iMessage unique to mastering the art of emoticon use and creating lively group chats, this chapter is your guide to becoming an iMessage expert.

What is iMessage and How It Differs from SMS

iMessage, a vital part of Apple's ecosystem, **is a messaging service that stands apart from the traditional Short Message Service (SMS) in several ways.** It provides a richer and more dynamic messaging experience, promoting smooth communication among iPhone and Apple device users.

iMessage relies on an internet connection to transmit messages, enabling quicker and more efficient communication, especially when connected to Wi-Fi. Messages sent via iMessage are represented by **blue chat bubbles**, making it easy to recognize the messaging platform in use. iMessage excels in sharing multimedia, allowing users to send high-quality photos, videos, audio messages, documents, and animated GIFs without compromising quality. It also offers read receipts, indicating when a recipient has read a message, enhancing communication transparency. With end-to-end encryption, iMessage ensures the privacy and security of your messages. However, it is exclusive to Apple devices, offering seamless integration with other Apple services and apps.

> *Pro Tip: Implement third-party iMessage apps and extensions to enhance your messaging experience. These apps provide advanced features like collaborative document editing, file sharing, and interactive widgets within iMessage conversations.*

How to Activate and Use iMessage

Activating iMessage is a simple process. **Just open the "Settings" on your iOS device, scroll down to "Messages," and toggle on the iMessage switch.**

Once activated, iMessage seamlessly takes the place of SMS as the default messaging platform when communicating with other Apple device users.

To send an iMessage, compose a message as usual, but instead of seeing green chat bubbles, you'll see blue ones, indicating that you're using iMessage.

Pro Tip: Develop custom iMessage apps and stickers using Apple's developer tools. This advanced customization allows you to create unique interactive experiences within iMessage for personal or business use.

Using emojis: what they are and how they can enrich conversations

Emojis are the universal language of the digital age, allowing users to convey emotions, reactions, and sentiments in a fun and visual way. **With iMessage, you have access to a vast library of emoticons to enhance your conversations.** Emoticons inject personality and style into your messages, making them more engaging and expressive. Whether you're sending a smiley face, a thumbs-up, or a heart, emoticons enable you to communicate beyond words.

Pro Tip: Incorporate shortcuts and text replacements for frequently used emojis and symbols. This streamlines your emoji input and allows for complex emoji combinations with a few keystrokes.

Creating Group Chats and Naming Groups

iMessage offers the convenience of forming and participating in group chats, enabling you to communicate with multiple contacts at once.

To create a group chat, open iMessage, tap the "+" icon, and add multiple recipients. You can also give the group a name for easy identification. Group chats are perfect for planning events, collaborating on projects, or simply staying in touch with a group of friends.

Pro Tip: Set up automated group chat management using shortcuts. You can create advanced rules for group membership, message forwarding, and even scheduled group announcements.

Access to Emoticons

Reacting to Messages with "Tapback"

"Tapback" is a handy feature that lets you react to messages with a simple tap and hold. You can choose from various reactions like thumbs-up, thumbs-down, laughter, and more. This feature adds an interactive and playful dimension to your conversations, allowing for quick responses without typing.

> *Pro Tip: Extend Tapback functionality with automation scripts that trigger specific actions based on received Tapback reactions. This adds a layer of automation to your messaging interactions.*

Sharing Photos, Videos, and Documents through iMessage

iMessage simplifies the sharing of multimedia. **You can send high-quality photos, videos, and documents directly within the chat. To share media, tap the camera icon for photos and videos or the document icon for files.** This seamless integration makes it easy to share memories, work-related documents, and more.

> *Pro Tip: Explore automation workflows that automatically organize and tag incoming media from iMessage conversations. These workflows can integrate with cloud storage services for seamless media management.*

Creating a Sticker from a Photo in Your Gallery

iMessage offers a creative feature that lets you transform your photos into stickers. **Open a conversation, tap the App Store icon, select "Photos," and choose a picture.** You can then customize the sticker by resizing it and adding text or emoticons. These personalized stickers add a unique touch to your messages.

Voice Messages with iMessage

Sometimes, conveying your thoughts through voice is more effective than text. iMessage allows you to send voice messages with ease. Simply press and hold the microphone icon, record your message, and release it to send. This feature is perfect for conveying tone and emotion in your conversations.

With iMessage, your messaging experience goes beyond the ordinary. From its dynamic multimedia capabilities to the playful world of emoticons and the convenience of group chats, iMessage empowers you to communicate in a way that reflects your personality and style. Dive into this chapter to unlock the full potential of iMessage and make your conversations come alive.

4.3 Sharing Your Location

In this segment, we'll delve into the robust features Apple provides for sharing your whereabouts with loved ones and pals. Whether your aim is to make sure your dear ones stay informed about your location in real-time or to create a more organized and connected family environment, Apple's tools have got you covered.

How to share your real-time location with family or friends

Apple has streamlined the process of sharing your live location with family or friends directly from your iOS gadget. Here's how to go about it:

 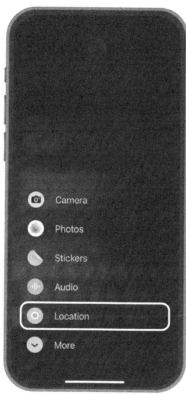 

1. **Open Messages**: Launch the **Messages app** on your iPhone or iPad.

2. **Choose a Chat**: Opt for the chat with the individual you wish to share your location with or initiate a fresh conversation.

3. **Tap on "+ " icon**: then tap Share. Or **Tap the name of the person** you want to share your location at the top of the conversation.

4. **Share Your Location**: Tap Location or Share My Location.

5. **Set a Time Limit**: If you opt for a limited duration, your location-sharing cease automatically when chosen time elapses.

6. **Confirmation**: A message is dispatched to the recipient, notifying them that you're sharing your location.

This feature proves incredibly handy for rendezvousing with friends, ensuring your family knows you're safe, or coordinating real-time plans.

> *Pro Tip: Integrate location data into third-party apps and services through APIs. This advanced usage allows you to create custom location-based experiences or analytics.*

Setting Up and Benefits of Family Sharing

Apple's Family Sharing function is designed to simplify the sharing of your preferred apps, tunes, and more with your family members. It offers a terrific way to keep everyone connected while preserving individual Apple IDs. Here's how to set it up and some of the perks it offers:

1. **Open Settings**: Navigate to the **Settings app** on your device.

2. **Tap Your Apple ID**: Usually found at the top of the screen.

3. **Family Sharing**: Click on **"Family Sharing"** and adhere to the on-screen directions to configure it.

Some of the principal advantages of Family Sharing include:

- **Shared Purchases**: Share your App Store and iTunes acquisitions with your family. This means you only need to purchase apps, music, and films once, and everybody in the family can enjoy them.

- **Family Calendar**: Craft a shared family calendar where all can contribute events and appointments. This simplifies keeping track of one another's schedules.

- **Find My iPhone**: Effortlessly locate any family member's device using the Find My app. This comes in handy, especially if a device is lost or pilfered.

- **Screen Time**: Parents can impose Screen Time constraints on their children's devices, ensuring they don't spend an excessive amount of time on screens.

- **Ask to Buy**: For younger family members, you can activate "Ask to Buy," requiring them to obtain approval before procuring apps or making in-app acquisitions.

Pro Tip: Develop custom apps or widgets that leverage Family Sharing data for family-oriented services or utilities, enhancing the overall family sharing experience.

Creating a Family Calendar

A shared family calendar proves invaluable for maintaining everybody's organization and coordination. Here's how to establish one:

1. **Open the Calendar App**: Open the **Calendar app** on your iOS device.

2. **Select "Calendars"**: At the screen's bottom, choose **"Calendars."**

3. **Tap "Add Calendar**:" in the lower left-hand corner twice.

4. **Type a name for the new calendar**: Make sure the account type is iCloud & tap Done.

Once you are done creating your shared iCloud calendar, follow these steps to add a person on your Family Calendar.

1. **Tap on "Calendars"**: at the bottom of your Apple Calendar app:

2. **Tap the Info button**: next to the iCloud calendar you want to share:

3. **Tap Add person**: to add any other members to your calendar, you will need to have their email to do so:

4. **Pubblic Calendar**: toggle on Pubblic Calendar

5. **Tap on Share Link**: to send it to family members.

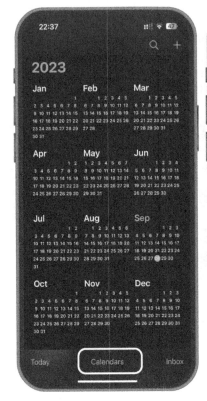
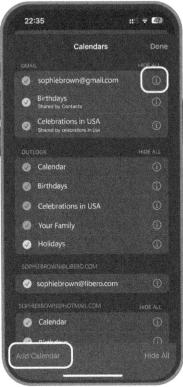

Now, everyone in your family can insert and modify events, making certain all remain informed about significant dates and appointments.

Pro Tip: Implement third-party family calendar apps that offer advanced scheduling features, such as automated event creation based on family members' schedules or location-based reminders.

Using "Ask to Buy" for Younger Family Members

For families containing younger members possessing their own Apple IDs, enabling "Ask to Buy" is a valuable feature. It necessitates parents or guardians to approve or reject app purchases and in-app transactions initiated by the child's Apple ID. Here's how to arrange it:

1. **Open Settings**: Access the **Settings app** on your device.

2. **Select Your Apple ID**: Frequently positioned at the top of the screen.

3. **Explore Family Sharing**: Pick **"Family Sharing."**

4. **Incorporate a Family Member**: Choose the child for whom you desire to activate "Ask to Buy."

5. **Enable "Ask to Buy"**: Turn on the "Ask to Buy" toggle.

With "Ask to Buy" enabled, when the child endeavors to make a purchase, a notification is conveyed to the parent or guardian's device. They can then endorse or decline the request, guaranteeing that acquisitions are executed with authorization.These features simplify the process of sharing your location, managing your family's digital existence, and ensuring that everyone stays organized and connected. Whether it's synchronizing meetups, distributing app acquisitions, or securing your child's online activities, Apple's tools are up to the task.

Pro Tip: Integrate "Ask to Buy" functionality into parental control apps, providing granular control over app purchase approvals and usage monitoring.

4.4 FaceTime

In this section, we'll plunge into the universe of FaceTime, Apple's iconic video calling platform. FaceTime altered the way we connect with pals and family, offering seamless video and audio calls that bridge geographical gaps. We'll explore the fundamentals, advanced features, and accessibility options to ensure everyone can savor the enchantment of FaceTime.

Introduction to Video Calls with FaceTime

FaceTime, presented by Apple, brought video calling into the mainstream. It's a feature-packed platform that permits you to engage in video and audio dialogues with acquaintances and family, no matter their global location. FaceTime is celebrated for its outstanding video and audio quality, making it a top preference for staying linked with cherished ones.

> *Pro Tip: Implement FaceTime API integrations into custom apps or services for specialized video communication solutions, such as telemedicine or virtual events.*

Using FaceTime for Audio or Video Calls

FaceTime is adaptable, enabling both audio and video calls. Here's how to commence:

1. **Open FaceTime**: Initiate the **FaceTime app** on your iOS tool or Mac.

2. **Choose a Contact**: Tap the "+" **icon** or look up a contact's name or number.

3. **Pick the Call Type**: Opt for a video call by tapping the video camera icon or an audio call via the phone icon.

4. **Initiate the Call**: Tap the call icon to initiate the call. Your contact receives an invite to join.

5. **Enjoy Your Call**: Once the call is connected, you can converse as if you were in the same place.

Pro Tip: Develop FaceTime plugins or extensions for specific industries, such as virtual education or remote collaboration, to enhance FaceTime's capabilities for professional use.

Creating FaceTime Groups

FaceTime grants you the capacity to construct group calls with multiple participants. Here's the procedure:

1. **Activate FaceTime**: Start the **FaceTime app.**

2. **Initiate a Fresh Call:** Tap the **"New Facetime"** icon to craft a new call.

3. **Add Participants**: Type the names or numbers of the people you want to call in the entry field at the top. You can also tap the "+" **button** to open Contacts and add people from there. Or tap suggested contacts in your call history. You can incorporate up to 32 participants in a group call.

4. **Start the Call**: Tap the call icon to commence the group call.

5. **Manage Participants**: While on the call, you can observe all participants on the screen. You also have the liberty to append more participants or eliminate them as required.

Pro Tip: Explore third-party FaceTime group management tools that offer advanced features like automatic participant invitation, scheduling, and recording for business or large-scale virtual events.

Transferring Calls Between Devices

One of Apple's exceptional characteristics is the ability to shift a call between devices without disruption. For instance, if you commence a call on your iPhone and wish to continue it on your Mac or iPad, here's the way:

1. **Start the Call**: Commence the call on one device.

2. **Seek the Handoff Icon**: If you have another compatible device nearby (signed in with the same Apple ID), a handoff icon becomes visible on the lock screen or in the dock.

3. **Swipe Up or Tap**: On your alternative device, either swipe up on the handoff icon (on iPhone) or tap it (on iPad or Mac). The call transfers smoothly, allowing you to switch devices seamlessly.

> *Pro Tip: Develop custom handoff solutions using Apple's Handoff APIs to seamlessly transfer FaceTime calls between not only Apple devices but also cross-platform devices and services.*

Call Continuity Across iPhone, iPad, and Mac

In Apple's ecosystem, you can fluidly transition among iPhone, iPad, and Mac during a FaceTime call. This continuity demonstrates Apple's dedication to user ease. You can inaugurate a call on one device and effortlessly transition to another while maintaining an uninterrupted call.

> *Pro Tip: Explore the development of custom call continuity solutions for specialized use cases, such as unified communications platforms that integrate with existing corporate phone systems.*

Accessibility Settings inCalls

Apple places strong emphasis on inclusivity, ensuring that its products accommodate users with diverse requirements. FaceTime boasts an array of accessibility settings to cater to individuals with varying needs. These settings encompass alternatives for enlarged text, voice commands, and more.

> *Pro Tip: Create custom accessibility scripts and extensions that extend the capabilities of FaceTime's accessibility settings. These scripts can integrate with assistive technologies and offer tailored accessibility solutions.*

In the sphere of video and audio calls, FaceTime stands as an emblem of how technology can bridge geographical separations, enabling meaningful interactions regardless of location. FaceTime provides a reliable and user-friendly platform for video and audio communication.

Chapter 5:

Photos and Videos

In this chapter, we will embark on a journey through the realm of photography and videography with your iPhone. Apple's Camera app has evolved over the years, offering a suite of features that cater to both beginners and seasoned photographers. We'll delve into the Camera app's interface, explore various shooting modes, and provide insights into maximizing your iPhone's camera capabilities.

5.1 Getting to know the Camera App

Overview of the Camera App Interface

The Camera app's interface is designed to be user-friendly and intuitive. Upon opening the app, you'll encounter a clean layout featuring several key components:

1.   Shutter Button: Located at the bottom of the screen, this prominent circular icon serves to capture photos or initiate video recording when tapped.

2.   Camera Modes: Swipe horizontally to switch between distinct camera modes, such as Photo, Video, Portrait, Panorama, and more. Each mode offers its own unique features and settings.

3.   Zoom Control: By pinching the viewfinder, you can zoom in or out. On newer iPhone models, you can achieve up to 3x optical zoom for closer shots.

4.   Flash: The lightning bolt icon allows you to adjust flash settings, typically offering options like Auto, On, and Off. Auto

CAMERA APP

mode automatically determines whether flash is needed based on the lighting conditions.

5.   HDR: Represented by an "HDR" icon, this feature enhances photo quality by capturing a range of exposures and merging them for a well-balanced shot. You can toggle it on or off as needed.

6.   Live Photos: If supported on your device, Live Photos capture a few seconds of video before and after taking a photo. You can enable or disable this feature using the circular "LIVE" icon.

7.   Timer: Recognizable as a stopwatch icon, the timer feature enables you to set a delay for capturing photos, particularly useful for group shots or selfies without the need to rush.

Pro Tip: Dive into advanced camera apps from the App Store that offer manual controls for settings like ISO, shutter speed, and focus. These apps provide professional-level photography capabilities.

FLASH   **TIMER**   **LIVE PHOTO**

Different Camera Modes

The Camera app offers an array of shooting modes tailored to various scenarios:

- **Photo**: The default mode for capturing standard photos.

- **Video**: Record high-quality videos with flexibility in resolutions and frame rates.

- **Portrait**: Ideal for capturing captivating portraits with a blurred background (bokeh effect).

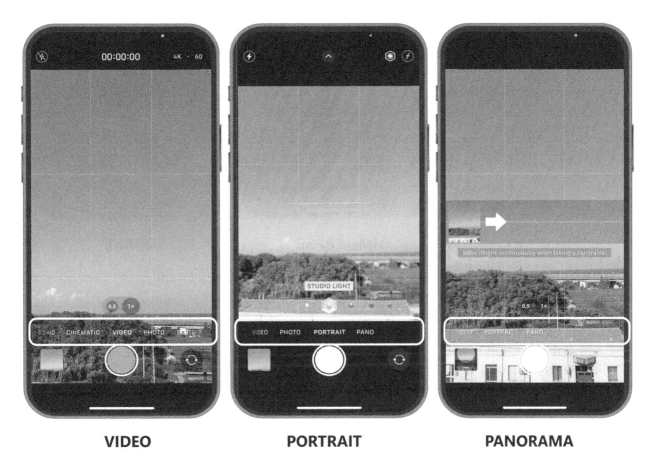

| VIDEO | PORTRAIT | PANORAMA |

- **Panorama**: Craft sweeping, wide-angle landscape shots.

- **Slo-mo**: Capture compelling slow-motion videos.

- **Time-lapse**: Record time-lapse videos, condensing hours into seconds.

- **Square**: Capture photos in a square format, perfect for social media.

| SLO-MO | TIME-LAPSE | SQUARE |

- **Night mode**: Enhance low-light photography by automatically adjusting exposure and shutter speed.

Pro Tip: Explore third-party camera apps that unlock additional shooting modes and features not available in the native Camera app. These apps offer creative options like long-exposure photography and time-lapse videos.

Zoom: How to use it when appropriate

Zoom functionality empowers you to get closer to your subject, but it should be employed judiciously. On newer iPhones, optical zoom offers clarity, while digital zoom may result in some loss of detail.Here's how to utilize zoom effectively:

- **Pinch to Zoom**: On the viewfinder, pinch inward to zoom out and pinch outward to zoom in, accompanied by a zoom level indicator.

- **Zoom for Detail**: Zoom aids in capturing intricate details or framing your subject more effectively, making it ideal for close-up shots of objects, architecture, or distant subjects.

- **Avoid Over-Zooming**: In low-light conditions, especially, steer clear of excessive zooming, which can lead to grainy or blurry photos.

Pro Tip: Invest in external lenses for your iPhone to achieve optical zoom capabilities and enhance image quality when zooming. These lenses attach to your iPhone for versatile photography.

Flash: Timing and Best Practices

The flash is a valuable tool for low-light photography, but its prudent application is pivotal for favorable outcomes. Here's when and how to use it:

- **Low-Light Settings**: Utilize the flash when faced with dimly lit environments, such as indoor or nighttime scenarios.

- **Fill Flash**: Occasionally, deploy the flash to mitigate shadows on your subject's face, especially when shooting outdoors in bright conditions.

- **Correct Harsh Light**: To soften the flash's impact, consider diffusing it with a tissue or dedicated diffuser accessory.

Pro Tip: Combine external flash units with your iPhone for studio-quality lighting control. External flashes provide more advanced lighting options for professional photography.

Timer: How to set and use it

The timer proves advantageous for capturing photos without necessitating another person to press the shutter button. Here's how to configure and employ it:

- **Activate the Timer Icon**: In the Camera app, locate and tap the timer icon, typically resembling a stopwatch.

- **Select the Delay**: Choose the desired delay time, often set at 3 or 10 seconds.

- **Initiate the Shutter**: After configuring the timer, press the shutter button. Subsequently, a countdown ensues, culminating in the automatic capture of the photo.

Pro Tip: Experiment with intervalometer apps that enable advanced time-lapse photography and automated shooting sequences. These apps offer precise control over timing and exposure settings.

By acquainting yourself with the Camera app's interface, diverse shooting modes, and mastering features like zoom, flash, and the timer, you'll be well-prepared to capture a plethora of moments with your iPhone's camera. Whether you're framing a picturesque landscape, encapsulating an impromptu portrait, or embarking on an exhilarating video journey, your iPhone's camera serves as a versatile instrument for nurturing your creative vision and immortalizing cherished memories.

5.2 Taking Photos Like a Pro

In this section, we'll dive deeper into the realm of iPhone photography, where the aim is not just to capture moments but to do so with finesse, creativity, and an eye for detail. We'll delve into essential techniques, settings, and features that will elevate your photography skills and enable you to take photos with the expertise of a professional.

Composition: The Rule of Thirds and Alignment

Composition serves as the cornerstone of exceptional photography. It's all about how you arrange the elements within your frame to craft an engaging and visually captivating image. Two fundamental composition principles are the "Rule of Thirds" and alignment.

- **Rule of Thirds**: Visualize dividing your photo into a grid of nine equal sections, akin to a tic-tac-toe board. The intersections of these lines are known as "hotspots." Positioning your subject or key elements near these hotspots can yield a balanced and aesthetically pleasing composition.

- **Alignment**: Pay careful attention to the alignment of your subject and other elements. Horizontal and vertical lines can serve as guides for the viewer's gaze. For instance, when photographing a sunset, aligning the horizon with one of the horizontal lines creates a harmonious composition.

Pro Tip: Study advanced composition principles like the Fibonacci spiral, leading diagonals, and the golden ratio for more sophisticated and visually engaging compositions.

Using Light: Making the Most of Natural and Artificial Lighting

Lighting stands as one of the paramount factors in photography. Proficiency in utilizing both natural and artificial light can significantly influence the outcome of your photos.

- **Natural Light**: When it comes to outdoor photography, the "golden hours" during sunrise and sunset bathe your subjects in soft, warm light that enhances their appeal. Overcast days provide diffused light with minimal harsh shadows.

- **Artificial Light**: In situations where you're shooting indoors or in settings with limited light, consider employing supplementary lighting sources like lamps or studio lights. Experiment with diverse angles and intensities to create the desired ambiance.

Pro Tip: Explore advanced lighting techniques, such as light painting and off-camera flash photography, to create dramatic and artistic lighting effects in your photos.

Focusing and blurring: how to focus on a subject and use depth of field

Precise focusing is essential to ensure that your subject appears sharp and well-defined. The iPhone's autofocus system is highly proficient, but you also have the option of taking manual control.

- **Autofocus**: A simple tap on your subject within the Camera app initiates autofocus. You'll observe a yellow box indicating the focal point.

- **Manual Focus**: For greater control, you can opt for manual focus. Tap your subject and then swipe your finger upward or downward to adjust the exposure. This, in turn, influences the focus, allowing you to intentionally introduce blurring or "bokeh" in the background.

Pro Tip: Invest in lens attachments that provide manual focus control, enabling precise focus adjustments for creative effects like bokeh and tilt-shift.

HDR: what it is and when to use it

HDR (High Dynamic Range) is a technique that combines multiple exposures of a scene to capture a broader spectrum of light and detail. It proves invaluable in scenarios characterized by high contrast, such as landscapes featuring a luminous sky and shadowed foreground.

- **Optimal Times for HDR**: Activate the HDR mode when you encounter scenes that encompass both brightly illuminated and dimly lit regions. The iPhone's HDR mode adeptly captures multiple exposures and merges them, yielding a well-balanced image.

Pro Tip: Use HDR apps with manual bracketing to capture high dynamic range scenes with maximum control over exposure. You can merge multiple exposures for HDR results.

Filters and effects: exploring and using built-in filters

The iPhone boasts a variety of built-in filters and effects that can infuse creativity and style into your photos. Feel free to experiment with these options to enrich your images:

- **Applying Filters**: Within the Camera app, **tapping the icon comprising three interlocking circles provides access to filters.** Swipe either left or right to preview and select the filter that best complements your photo.

Pro Tip: Experiment with advanced filter apps that offer customizable filter presets and layering options for more complex and artistic photo editing.

Creating albums and organizing photos

As your photo collection grows, maintaining organization assumes paramount importance. Establishing albums facilitates the categorization and efficient management of your photos:

- **Creating an Album**: **In the Photos app, navigate to "Albums," then tap the "+" icon to generate a new album.** Bestow upon it an appropriate name and incorporate chosen photos.

- **Arranging Photos**: Within albums, you have the flexibility to reposition photos according to your preference by employing the drag-and-drop method.

Pro Tip: Employ professional photo management software to catalog and organize your photo library, complete with metadata tagging and advanced search capabilities

What is a Live Photo and how to capture it

Live Photos infuse vitality into your pictures by capturing a few seconds of motion and sound preceding and succeeding the act of taking a photo:

- **Capturing a Live Photo**: Within the Camera app, confirm that **"Live" is activated (indicated by a yellow icon)**. Proceed to take a photo as usual, and it will automatically morph into a Live Photo.

Pro Tip: Use third-party apps that extend Live Photo functionality, allowing you to extract high-quality still frames from Live Photos and create cinemagraphs.

Editing and interacting with Live Photos

Live Photos can undergo edits and customizations to align with your preferences:

- **Editing**: Open a Live Photo in the Photos app and tap **"Edit."** Here, you can fine-tune aspects such as **cropping**, **brightness**, and the application of **filters**. You're also able to select an alternative keyframe from the Live Photo.

- **Effects**: Venture into the **"Effects" section** to experiment with **animations** like **Loop**, **Bounce**, or **Long Exposure**, imparting dynamic qualities to your Live Photos.

Pro Tip: Dive into advanced video editing software to harness the full potential of Live Photos, including video stabilization, color grading, and audio enhancements.

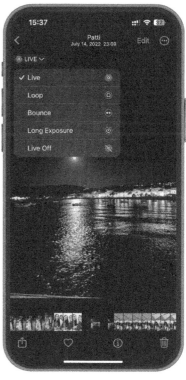

Portrait Mode: taking photos with blurred backgrounds

Portrait Mode leverages depth-sensing technology to yield professionally styled photos adorned with an artful background blur, commonly referred to as "bokeh":

- **Enabling Portrait Mode**: In the Camera app, navigate to "Portrait," frame your subject, and witness the automatic background blurring, which accentuates your subject.

Pro Tip: Utilize third-party apps that offer more extensive post-processing control over Portrait Mode photos, allowing for precise background blurring adjustments.

PORTRAIT MODE

RED EYE CORRECTION

Using the "Retouch" and "Red-eye correction" functions

The Photos app offers two valuable editing functions:

- **Retouch**: This functionality empowers you to eliminate blemishes or imperfections from your photos. Open the photo in question, tap "Edit," access the "Retouch" feature, and proceed to brush over the area necessitating retouching.

- **Red-Eye Correction**: In instances where a photo has been marred by red-eye occurrences induced by the flash, the Photos app steps in to perform automatic correction. Open the afflicted photo, access "Edit," select "Red-eye," and subsequently rectify each red-eye issue through tapping.

Pro Tip: Master advanced retouching techniques using professional-level photo editing software, enabling detailed and non-destructive retouching of portraits and images.

With these advanced photography techniques and insights, you're well on your way to mastering the art of iPhone photography. Photography is an artistic endeavor, and practice serves as the catalyst for enhancing your skills. Embark on a journey of experimentation, navigating through different settings, lighting scenarios, and compositions, to cultivate your unique style and capture moments with the finesse of a professional.

5.3 Recording Videos

In this segment, we plunge into the domain of video recording with your iPhone. Whether you're preserving life's unforgettable instances or unearthing your imaginative side, mastering video recording can aid in the narration of riveting tales. We will delve into pivotal methodologies, attributes, and recommendations to enhance your video recording adeptness.

Starting and stopping a video recording

The process of capturing videos on your iPhone adheres to a straightforward protocol.

Open the Camera: Unveil the Camera app on your iPhone.

1. **Transition to Video Mode**: Swipe the camera mode selector to opt for the "Video" alternative.

2. **Start Recording**: Tap the crimson recording button to embark on the video capture.

3. **End Recording**: To conclude the recording, re-tap the crimson button. Your video shall be automatically preserved within your Photos app.

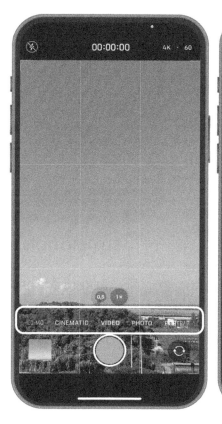

VIDEO   **RECORDING**

Pro Tip: Use external Bluetooth remotes or wireless camera control apps to initiate and conclude video recordings remotely. This ensures seamless transitions in your footage without the need to physically touch the device.

Slow-motion and time-lapse videos: how and when to use them

Your iPhone introduces inventive video modes that transcend the realms of conventional recording:

- **Slow-Motion**: Slow-motion videos encapsulate moments in a leisurely manner. They are ideal for accentuating brisk motions or fabricating theatrical effects.

To record in slow motion, direct your course towards the "Slo-Mo" mode, and press the crimson recording button. The velocity of the slow-motion effect can be adjusted during the subsequent editing phase.

- **Time-Lapse**: Time-lapse videos compress extended durations into succinct, visually captivating snippets.

To initiate the recording of a time-lapse video, glide towards the "Time-Lapse" mode and tap the crimson recording button. Your iPhone shall autonomously capture frames at specified intervals, resulting in a seamless time-lapse video.

SLO-MOTION　　　　　　　**TIME-LAPSE**

Zooming Whilst Recording: Nuggets of Wisdom and Tactical Maneuvers

The iPhone extends the privilege of zooming in or out during the recording of a video, thus presenting an array of dynamic framing prospects:

- **Zooming In**: For zooming in, employ the pinch gesture on the screen. Exercise prudence in executing smooth and gradual zooms to preserve video integrity. Alternatively, you may

manipulate the volume buttons to orchestrate zoom operations.

• **Zooming Out**: To effectuate a zoom-out action, engage in a reverse pinch gesture on the screen. Once again, adherence to a steady, progressive zoom is advocated for optimal outcomes.

Pro Tip: Dive into video editing software to apply frame interpolation techniques for ultra-smooth slow-motion videos. For time-lapses, consider using motorized sliders or gimbals for precise and controlled camera movements.

ZOOM IN

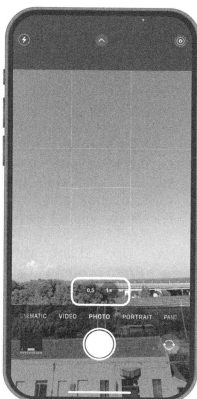

ZOOM OUT

Adjusting brightness, contrast, and other parameters

The camera app of your iPhone furnishes real-time adjustments, thereby elevating the caliber of your video:

• **Exposure Control**: While in the midst of recording, you possess the capability to fine-tune the exposure by tapping the screen. This action activates a sun icon, affording you the latitude to slide your finger upwards or downwards to manipulate brightness.

• **Exposure Lock**: In situations necessitating unwavering exposure, a long tap on the screen is warranted. Hold until the "AE/AF Lock" indicator materializes. This phenomenon secures both exposure and focus until a subsequent tap on the screen is executed to disengage it.

• **Focus Regulation**: Similar to exposure, focus can be manually adjusted by tapping on the screen. Execute a vertical slide of your finger upwards or downwards to attain the desired focus.

- **White Balance**: Although white balance is typically entrusted to the iPhone's automatic control, you possess the prerogative to assume manual authority for creative purposes. Initiate a tap on the screen to unveil the sun icon and subsequently execute a horizontal swipe to finesse the white balance.

Pro Tip: Shoot videos in RAW format using specialized camera apps for more extensive post-processing control. RAW video files preserve the highest quality data, allowing for advanced adjustments in professional video editing software.

EXPOSURE LOCK

EXPOSURE CONTROL

These video recording techniques and attributes empower you to encapsulate cinematic instants, dabble in artistic effects, and acclimatize to diverse shooting conditions. As you embark on your journey into the realm of video recording, take cognizance that honing your skills through consistent practice is pivotal in your quest to narrate enthralling visual chronicles with your iPhone.

5.4 Front Camera and Selfies

In this section, we shall delve into the capabilities of the front-facing camera on your iPhone, often employed for taking self-portraits, commonly known as selfies. We will explore strategies for capturing impeccable self-portraits, employing portrait mode for added depth and flair, and indulging in a touch of amusement with Animoji and Memoji.

Tips for taking perfect selfies

Selfies have assumed a ubiquitous role in self-expression, and with your iPhone's front camera, you wield a potent tool. Here are some recommendations to assist you in capturing the flawless self-portrait:

1.   **Illumination Matters**: Illumination plays a pivotal role in photography, and selfies are no exception. Typically, natural light is the most flattering. Therefore, situating yourself in proximity to a window or well-illuminated surroundings is advisable. Exercise caution when confronted with intense, direct sunlight, as it can give rise to uncomplimentary shadows.

2.   **Angles Count**: Experiment with various angles to pinpoint your preferred side. A marginally elevated camera angle can accentuate your features and impart the illusion of larger eyes.

3.   **Rule of Thirds**: Apply the rule of thirds by positioning your visage marginally off-center within the frame. This stratagem can introduce depth and visual allure into your self-portrait.

4.   **A Steady Hand**: Maintain steadiness in your hand to avert blurry photographs. You may utilize your iPhone's volume buttons as an alternative to screen tapping when capturing a photo.

5.   **Portrait Mode**: In the event that your iPhone furnishes support for portrait mode with the front camera, leverage it to conjure up self-portraits that emanate a professional aura, complete with a softly blurred backdrop.

6.   **Prudent Editing**: Post-selfie capture, contemplate employing photo editing applications to augment the image. Tweaking brightness, contrast, and color enables the attainment of the desired aesthetic without succumbing to excess.

7.   **Unleash Creativity**: Abandon inhibitions and embark on experimentation with assorted expressions, poses, and locales. Selfies are a manifestation of personal expression, and this is your opportunity to bask in the limelight of creativity.

Pro Tip: Explore Advanced Editing Apps: After taking your selfie, use professional photo editing apps to fine-tune details like skin texture, lighting, and colors. These apps provide precise control over your selfie's final look, ensuring flawless results.

Using portrait mode with the front camera

Portrait mode stands out as an exceptional attribute accessible on numerous contemporary iPhones. It possesses the potential to elevate your self-portraits to unprecedented heights. Below is a step-by-step guide for deploying it with the front camera:

1.   **Camera App Unveiling**: Commence by launching the **Camera app** on your iPhone.

2.   **Portrait Mode Activation**: A horizontal swipe to the **"Portrait" mode** is the next step.

3.   **Frame Your Shot**: Situate yourself or your subject within the frame and ensure an

adequate gap between you and the backdrop.

4. Focus Adjustment via Tap: Employ a tap on your countenance to convey your focus preferences to the camera. This gesture shall be accompanied by the appearance of a yellow box that demarcates the focal point.

5. Portrait Capture: The shutter button shall be depressed to commit your portrait to memory. The camera shall deploy depth information to create an exquisite backdrop blur, thereby conferring a striking visual effect.

6. Post-Capture Enhancements: Subsequent to portrait capture, you are at liberty to indulge in further editing. This includes tailoring the extent of background blur or applying filters to suit your preferences.

Pro Tip: Manual Control with Third-party Apps: Consider using third-party camera apps that offer manual control over Portrait Mode settings.

This level of control allows you to adjust aperture, focal length, and depth effects for highly customized front-camera portraits.

| PORTRAIT | FOCAL POINT |

Animoji and Memoji: having fun with the front camera

Your iPhone ushers in an element of amusement through Animoji and Memoji. These functionalities rely upon the front camera to map your facial expressions onto animated characters or personalized avatars.

1.   **Messages App Initiation**: Embark on your journey by launching the **Messages app** and initiating a conversation.

2.   **Accessing Animoji**: **Adjacent to the text input field, there is an App Store icon**; tap it. Subsequently, opt for the Animoji icon, typically depicted as a monkey.

3.   **Character Selection**: Delve into the array of **Animoji and Memoji characters** and make a selection in accordance with your fancy.

4.   **Recording Your Message**: A tap on the crimson record button shall enable you to express yourself verbally or via facial gestures. The character you have chosen will mimic your actions and voice.

5.   **Message Dissemination**: Upon completion, dispatch your animated message by tapping the blue send button, thereby sharing your creation with your contacts.

Pro Tip: Animoji Storytelling: Take Animoji to the next level by creating short stories or skits using multiple Animoji characters. Plan and script your scenes for entertaining and creative Animoji videos.

By embarking on an exploration of the front camera and its innovative attributes, such as portrait mode and Animoji, you open the floodgates to added depth and entertainment in the realm of self-portraiture.

Whether your objective is the cultivation of professional-looking portraits or indulging in amusement via animated characters, your iPhone's front camera unveils an expanse of prospects for self-expression and imaginative expression.

ANIMOJI

Chapter 6:

Photo Gallery 🎤

Within this chapter, we embark on a journey through the Photo Gallery on your iPhone, a repository of your cherished memories immortalized in pixels. We'll explore how to efficiently traverse your photo collection, employ intelligent search to unearth specific moments, and unveil the wealth of insights concealed within each image.

6.1 Overview of the Photo Gallery

Your Photo Gallery serves as a visual journal, chronicling the moments, locations, and individuals that have enriched your life. Here's an all-encompassing examination of ways to navigate and maximize your Photo Gallery:

Navigating through photos:

View by days, months, years

1.   **Viewing by Timelines**: The Photo Gallery offers diverse methods for perusing your photos. You can peruse them chronologically by days, offering a timeline of your images. To achieve this, launch the **Photos app** and click on **"Photos"** at the bottom of the screen. Employ a swipe in the upward or downward direction to navigate through the days.

2.   **Smart Albums**: Your iPhone takes the initiative to arrange your photos into intelligent albums like **"Favorites,"** **"Live Photos,"** **"Videos,"** and **"Selfies."** These albums grant prompt access to particular photo types.

Pro Tip: Utilize machine learning features to let your iPhone automatically categorize and tag your photos based on people, places, and objects, making searching for specific photos even more effortless.

Smart search:

How to find photos based on place, date, or people

1. Places: For locating photos captured at a precise site, tap the "Search" icon in the Photos app and input the location, e.g., "Paris." Your iPhone will exhibit all photos taken in that locale.

2. Dates: You retain the capability to search for photos taken on a particular date or within a specified date range. Merely insert the date or date range into the search bar, and your iPhone will apply filters accordingly.

3. Individuals: Your iPhone employs facial recognition to identify faces in your photos, permitting you to search for images featuring specific individuals. Insert the individual's name into the search bar to view all photos containing their visage.

4. Objects and Scenes: iOS harnesses machine learning to detect objects and settings within your photos. As an instance, you can seek out "mountains" or "birthday," prompting your iPhone to present pertinent images.

Pro Tip: Explore advanced search queries using keywords and natural language to unearth specific photos from your extensive gallery quickly

Viewing photo information: date, location, and technical details

Every photo nestled within your gallery encapsulates a wealth of insights. Here's the pathway to access them:

1. **Dates**: Execute a tap on a photo to peruse it in full-screen mode. A swipe upwards on the screen unveils particulars concerning the photo, encompassing the date of capture.

2. **Locations**: Within the same view, you can also discern the site where the photo was taken, contingent on the activation of your camera's location services.

3. **Technical Details**: For those possessing an inclination for the technical facets of photography, a swipe in the downward direction will expose specifics such as the camera utilized, shutter speed, ISO, and more.

Your Photo Gallery surpasses the confines of a digital album; it functions as an instrument empowering you to reminisce, categorize, and retrieve cherished memories. By mastering the art of navigation, search proficiency, and data retrieval, you can unlock the complete potential of this invaluable asset.

Whether you're revisiting a getaway, hunting for the perfect shot, or simply reflecting on a special moment, your Photo Gallery serves as your portal to days gone by.

> *Pro Tip: Dive into the technical details of your photos and gain insights into exposure settings, camera equipment, and even the specific lens used for capturing each shot.*

6.2 Memories and photo sharing

Your iPhone isn't just a camera; it's a memory curator. In this chapter, we delve into the fascinating world of "Memories" and explore the art of sharing photos with family and friends. From automatic slideshows to crafting shared albums, your Photo Gallery is a dynamic hub for reliving and celebrating those significant moments.

What is the "Memories" section:

How iPhone automatically creates slideshows and albums

1. **Understanding "Memories"**: Memories is a unique feature on your iPhone that creates slideshows and albums automatically, based on important events, places, or timeframes in your life. Think of it as your personal digital historian.

2. **Customizing Your Memories**: While Memories are generated automatically, you have the flexibility to put your personal touch on them. Customize the title, music, and content of your Memories to make them uniquely yours.

3. **Enjoying Memory Movies**: Memories are not static; they come to life in Memory movies. These dynamic slideshows feature cinematic transitions and your selected background music.

Pro Tip: Customize the auto-generated Memories by creating your own custom categories and defining the criteria for selecting photos, giving you greater control over the narrative of your memories.

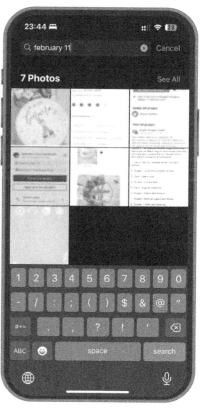

Customizing and editing Memories

1.   Sharing a Memory: Memories are best when shared. To share a Memory with family and friends, open the Memory, tap the "Share" icon, and choose your preferred method—like messaging, email, or social media.

Pro Tip: Go beyond basic editing and use advanced editing tools and techniques to create cinematic Memories with precise control over transitions, music, and visual effects.

Create and watch Memory movies

1.   Starting a Shared Album: Shared albums are an excellent way to collaborate with others and curate collections of photos and videos. Create a shared album by opening the Photos app, selecting "Albums," and tapping the **"+" icon.**

2.   Inviting Participants and Managing Notifications: When creating a shared album, invite participants by entering their email addresses. You can also tailor notification settings to stay informed about new additions.

3. Adding and Removing Content: Once a shared album is established, easily include photos and videos. Open the album, tap the **"+" icon**, and select the content you wish to include. Removing content is just as straightforward.

4. Commenting and Liking: Shared albums foster collaboration. You and your participants can leave comments on photos and videos, creating a dynamic and interactive experience. Show appreciation by liking shared content.

5. Saving Photos from Shared Albums: If you stumble upon a gem in a shared album that you'd like to keep in your own Gallery, you can save it to your device with a simple tap.

6. Exporting Photos and Videos: Occasionally, you may want to store photos and videos externally. Exporting content from shared albums simplifies saving them to your device or cloud storage.

Pro Tip: Explore third-party video editing apps to craft highly polished Memory Movies, complete with professional-grade effects and transitions. Implement a comprehensive digital asset management (DAM) system to efficiently catalog and archive your exported photos and videos, ensuring long-term accessibility and organization.

Your iPhone transcends its role as a mere photo-taking device; it becomes a vessel for creating, sharing, and revisiting precious memories. By mastering the art of Memories and photo sharing, you can weave a digital tapestry of memories that will be treasured for generations to come. Whether it's the nostalgia of a Memory slideshow or the collaborative spirit of a shared album, your iPhone empowers you to keep your cherished moments close to your heart and share them with those who matter most.

6.3 Using iCloud Photo Sharing

iCloud Photo Sharing elevates your photo-sharing capabilities to new heights. In this chapter, we'll delve into what iCloud Photo Sharing entails and how it sets itself apart from shared albums. You'll also grasp the process of enabling this feature in your iPhone settings, making photo and video sharing with connected devices effortless. Additionally, we'll explore effective management of your iCloud storage space and available purchase options, ensuring your treasured memories are consistently accessible.

What is iCloud Photo Sharing and how it differs from the shared album

1. **Defining iCloud Photo Sharing**: iCloud Photo Sharing is a feature designed for the seamless and organized sharing of your photos and videos. Unlike shared albums, which maintain a level of privacy and are accessible to specific invitees, iCloud Photo Sharing broadens your sharing horizons, allowing you to share your content with a wider audience, including friends and family using Apple devices.

2. **Distinguishing Factors from Shared Albums**: While shared albums focus on privacy and exclusivity, iCloud Photo Sharing extends your sharing reach to encompass a larger circle of contacts. It's particularly useful for sharing family photos, event snapshots, or vacation memories with a broader network.

Pro Tip: Integrate iCloud Photo Sharing with cloud-based AI services to automatically categorize and tag shared photos, enhancing searchability and organization.

Enable iCloud Photo Sharing in Settings

1. **Accessing Settings**: To activate iCloud Photo Sharing, initiate the **"Settings" app** on your iPhone.

2. **Your Apple ID**: Scroll down and select your name, situated at the top of the Settings page, to access your Apple ID settings.

3. **iCloud**: Inside your Apple ID settings, proceed by tapping **"iCloud."**

4. **Photos**: Scroll further down the page to locate the **"Photos" option.** Tapping it grants access to your iCloud Photos settings.

5. **Enabling iCloud Photo Sharing**: Engage the **"iCloud Photo Sharing"** toggle to activate this feature.

 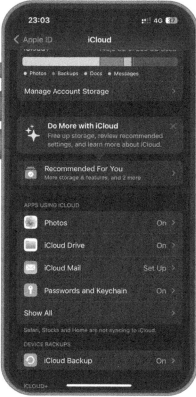 

Pro Tip: Implement advanced access control and permissions management for iCloud Photo Sharing, allowing you to fine-tune who can view, edit, and contribute to shared content.

Automatically share photos and videos with connected devices

1.   Universal Sharing: Following the activation of iCloud Photo Sharing, your photos and videos will undergo automatic synchronization across all your interconnected Apple devices. This seamless process ensures your content remains readily accessible on your iPhone, iPad, Mac, and other Apple products.

Pro Tip: Set up advanced synchronization and backup strategies using third-party cloud services in conjunction with iCloud Photo Sharing for redundancy and data resilience.

Manage iCloud storage space and purchase options

1.   Regularly Check iCloud Storage: It's prudent to regularly monitor your iCloud storage capacity as you continue capturing and sharing memories. Access this information by navigating to **"Settings"** > **[Your Name]** > **"iCloud"** > **"Manage Storage."**

2. Upgrade Opportunities: In the event of dwindling iCloud storage space, consider purchasing additional storage. Apple offers a range of storage plans to accommodate your requirements, guaranteeing secure storage of your photos and videos in the cloud.

Pro Tip: Implement data deduplication and compression techniques to optimize your iCloud storage utilization further, reducing costs and increasing storage efficiency.

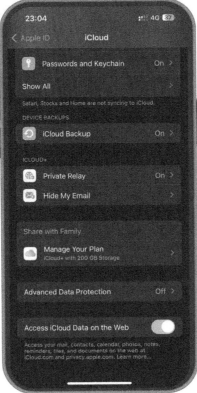

By harnessing the power of iCloud Photo Sharing, you establish a streamlined photo-sharing experience with your network of friends and family. It simplifies the process of sharing cherished memories, whether they pertain to a family gathering, a vacation escapade, or a special occasion.

With the ability to seamlessly share content across your suite of Apple devices, your photos and videos are perpetually within reach. Moreover, through astute management of your iCloud storage resources, you can ensure the safety and accessibility of your treasured memories.

6.4 Editing photos in the Gallery

In the digital era, photographs transcend mere captured moments; they serve as canvases for our creativity and self-expression. **The iPhone's Photo Gallery is a reservoir of your visual memories, and it doubles as a potent tool for enhancing and refining your photos.** This chapter delves into the realm of photo editing within the Gallery, encompassing both rudimentary and sophisticated tools that empower you to metamorphose your photos into captivating works of art.

Basic tools: cropping, rotation, and auto-correction

At the core of elementary photo editing reside fundamental tools capable of profoundly augmenting the composition and general quality of your photos. Cropping permits the elimination of undesired elements and the reorientation of the viewer's focus toward your subject.

The act of rotating a photo can rectify skewed horizons or reposition an image to achieve a sought-after perspective. Conversely, auto-correction leverages intelligent algorithms to automatically fine-tune exposure, contrast, and color balance, often resulting in more equilibrated and visually pleasing photos with a mere tap.

Pro Tip: Employ batch processing tools and scripts to apply consistent cropping, rotation, and auto-correction settings to large sets of photos for a cohesive look and feel.

CROPPING

AUTO-CORRECTION

Advanced Edits: Refinement of Brightness, Contrast, Saturation, and Beyond

For those with a penchant for comprehensive control over their photo edits, the Gallery offers an assortment of advanced adjustment tools. These tools bestow the capacity to meticulously fine-tune every facet of your image.

You can modulate brightness to illuminate dim areas or temper excessively bright sections, finetune contrast to accentuate particulars within your photo, and manipulate saturation to invigorate colors or imbue your image with a vintage ambiance.

Beyond these foundational adjustments, you can delve into alternatives such as shadows, highlights, and brilliance to attain the ideal aesthetic.

BRIGHTNESS   **CONTRAST**   **SATURATION**

Pro Tip: Develop custom presets and filters using photo editing software with scripting capabilities, allowing you to apply intricate adjustments across multiple photos effortlessly.

Filters: how to apply and which one to choose Application and Selection Criteria

Filters represent a creative shortcut for infusing your photos with **distinctive styles and atmospheres.** The Gallery bestows an array of filters, each possessing its unique aesthetic.

The application of a filter involves perusing the available options and selecting the one that best aligns with your creative vision. Filters can span from intensifying color vibrancy to incorporating vintage, monochromatic, or dramatic effects.

While filters can serve as an enjoyable and expedited means of transmuting your photos, remember that subtlety often yields the most striking outcomes.

FILTER

AUTO-CORRECTION

> *Pro Tip: Harness machine learning algorithms to analyze the visual content of your photos and suggest the most suitable filters based on the photo's subject and composition.*

Delete edits: return to the original photo

Innovation constitutes an integral facet of the creative process, and the Gallery appreciates this facet. If, at any juncture, you sense that your edits have ventured too far or simply wish to revert to the initial photo, apprehension is unwarranted. **The "Revert" function emerges as your ally. Situated within the editing interface, it affords you the ability to backtrack through your edits step by step, thereby affording complete authority over the ultimate appearance of your photo.**

> *Pro Tip: Implement version control and non-destructive editing workflows to preserve a comprehensive edit history while maintaining access to the original photo.*

Editing photos within the Gallery transcends the realm of rectifying imperfections; it epitomizes the liberation of your creativity and the transformation of your images into entrancing visual narratives. Equipped with rudimentary instruments, advanced refinements, and an assortment of filters, you possess the wherewithal to craft photos that reverberate with your distinct style and perspective. Thus, do not hesitate to embark on exploratory journeys, engage in experimentation, and refine your photos to engender digital masterpieces that manifest as truly distinguished creations.

6.5 Management and organization

In the digital epoch, our lives are exquisitely chronicled through photographs. These visual recollections enable us to rekindle cherished instants, partake in shared experiences, and foster connections with others. Nonetheless, as your iPhone's digital photo library burgeons, the apt management and organization of your gallery become paramount. In this section, we shall navigate the intricacies of photo administration and organization within your Gallery, aiding you in crafting a compilation that narrates your distinctive story.

Create custom albums and add photos

One of the primary steps in gallery management involves the creation of **customized albums.** These digital repositories afford you the capability to categorize your photographs, rendering them more accessible and enjoyable.

Whether the task involves the categorization of photographs by events, individuals, or themes, customized albums offer versatility.

To initiate the creation of an album, direct your attention to the "+" icon in your Gallery and opt for "New Album." Bestow a name upon it, and you stand prepared to populate it with photographs.

NEW ALBUM

ENTER A NAME

The act of adding photographs to an album transpires as a straightforward process, entailing the selection of said photographs and the subsequent choice of **"Add to Album."** This intuitive procedure empowers you to assemble a bespoke compilation tailored to your proclivities.

> *Pro Tip: Develop custom organizational scripts that automatically categorize and tag photos based on your preferred criteria, saving you significant time in managing your gallery.*

Hide photos or albums

While the act of memory-sharing exudes magnificence, occasions arise wherein you might aspire to confine particular photographs or albums to a private realm. The Gallery incorporates a functionality that permits the concealment of photographs or entire albums from the primary view.

The act of concealing a photograph entails its unveiling, the selection of the share button, and the subsequent designation of "Hide." **As for albums, you can obscure them by traversing to the "Albums" tab, executing a leftward swipe on the album slated for obscurity, and thereafter opting for "Hide."** This functionality guarantees that your private moments endure in a state of privacy.

> *Pro Tip: Implement advanced access controls and encryption techniques to secure hidden photos or albums, ensuring the utmost privacy and protection.*

Tag people in photos for easier searching

In the milieu of a sprawling digital photo library, the act of pinpointing particular photographs can, at times, mimic the search for a needle within a haystack. In a bid to streamline this procedure, the Gallery enables the affixation of tags to individuals within your photographs. The tagging of a person establishes an association between their name and the photograph, thereby facilitating its retrieval during searches.

The tagging process commences with the opening of a photograph, followed by the initiation of "Edit" in the upper-right corner, culminating in the selection of the "Add" button situated beneath "People." Subsequently, you can ascertain and tag individuals depicted within the photograph. Once tagged, the expedited location of photographs featuring specific individuals is feasible via a name-based search conducted within the Gallery's search bar.

Pro Tip: Utilize facial recognition

Favorites: how to mark and find your favorite photos

Not all photographs resonate to the same degree; certain ones bear profound significance. **The "Favorites" attribute within the Gallery provides you with the means to mark specific photographs as your favorites,** birthing a curated assortment of cherished moments.

The process of designating a photograph as a favorite involves its unveiling, followed by a tap upon the heart icon stationed at the lower section of the screen. **Once marked, your favored photographs become effortlessly accessible within the "Favorites" album.** This feature serves as a splendid avenue to assemble a personalized gallery comprised of moments held close to your heart.

Pro Tip: Implement machine learning algorithms that analyze your interaction patterns with photos to automatically mark and suggest favorites, streamlining the process.

The adept administration and organization of your digital photo gallery constitute an art form in and of itself.

Armed with the ability to contrive customized albums, conceal private photographs, tag individuals to expedite searches, and compile an anthology of favorites, your Gallery metamorphoses into a canvas whereupon you meticulously craft a visual saga of your existence.

Embrace these organizational instruments, cleanse your digital expanse, and facilitate the act of revisiting and disseminating your treasured memories amongst companions and family.

Your gallery transcends the mere collation of photographs; it embodies a chronicle of life's most precious instants.

6.6 Trash management

In the intricate mosaic of our digital existence, our photo galleries emerge as living archives of cherished instants. Nevertheless, amid the hustle and bustle of daily life and the continuous inflow of images, inadvertent deletions can transpire. Fear not, for the iPhone's Gallery encompasses a protective mechanism, a digital safety precaution recognized as the Trash. In this section, we shall delve into the method by which you can prudently delete photographs, recuperate those that have been unintentionally purged, and ensure the preservation of your digital recollections.

Safely delete photos and recover deleted photos

As time unfurls, your photo gallery accumulates a voluminous trove of images, several of which may have lost their significance. To liberate storage space and streamline your Gallery, it becomes imperative to acquaint yourself with the process of judiciously deleting photographs.

The deletion of a photograph transpires in a straightforward manner: upon its unveiling, direct your attention to the trash icon positioned in the lower-right corner, and subsequently, affirm

the act of deletion. However, it's imperative to bear in mind that deleted photographs are not instantaneously eradicated from your device.

Pro Tip: Implement advanced data recovery and forensic tools to securely and comprehensively erase sensitive photos, ensuring they are beyond recovery when deleted.

Recovering Deleted Photos: The Gallery's Safety Net

Mistakes Happen

Errors transpire, and it is not uncommon to eradicate a photograph, only to realize its necessity at a later juncture. In such instances, the Trash feature emerges as the savior.

When a photograph is deleted, it undergoes a process of relocation to the "Recently Deleted" album within the Gallery.

This album operates as a protective mesh, harboring your deleted photographs for a predetermined duration prior to their permanent elimination.

To resuscitate a deleted photograph, navigate to the "Recently Deleted" album, select the photograph slated for restoration, execute a tap upon "Recover," and presto, it is reinstated within your gallery.

Managing Your Safety Net: Emptying the Trash

Clearing the Digital Clutter

While the Trash operates as an invaluable safety precaution, periodic oversight is essential. **Deleted photographs are not automatically expunged from the "Recently Deleted" album, signifying that they continue to consume storage capacity.** In order to reclaim storage space

and irrevocably eradicate photographs from the Trash, steer your course towards the "Recently Deleted" album. Subsequently, **initiate the selection process by executing a tap upon "Select" located in the upper-right corner, followed by a further tap upon "Delete All"** positioned at the lower-left extremity. A confirmation dialogue shall ensue, seeking affirmation of your intention to irrevocably expunge these photographs. Once confirmed, the photographs shall be consigned to oblivion.

In the ceaselessly evolving digital realm, wherein recollections are progressively preserved through the optic lens of our devices, the effective administration of your photo gallery stands as an indispensable facet of safeguarding your cherished instants. Proficiency in the methods of prudently deleting photographs, recuperating those inadvertently erased, and astutely managing your digital safety mesh assures the endurance of your digital reminiscences, primed for revisitation and sharing with friends and family across the forthcoming years.

Chapter 7:

Internet, Email, and Online Safety 🎤

7.1 Introducing Safari: the gateway to the web

How to search for information and websites

Safari, your iPhone's dependable web browser, serves as the gateway to the expansive realm of the internet. To embark on your digital odyssey, it's imperative to grasp the art of sourcing information and accessing websites.

Safari

Swiftly accessing the Safari search bar grants you entry into this boundless reservoir of online knowledge.

Proficiency in this rudimentary skill is akin to possessing a key to the treasure trove of digital information.

Pro Tip: Capitalize on Safari's Smart Search bar, a versatile tool that serves both as your entry point for web searches and a portal for entering website addresses. This fusion of functionality is an invaluable time-saving feature for expeditiously locating desired content.

Use tabs and bookmarks

Tabs introduce a paradigm shift in the domain of web browsing, allowing for the simultaneous operation of multiple web pages, all within easy reach via a mere tap.

Mastery over tab management empowers you to multitask with precision and maintain a comprehensive overview of your online engagements. Complementing this, bookmarks function as your virtual shortcuts to favored websites.

Acquiring the skill to save, categorize, and systematically arrange bookmarks ensures that your preferred online destinations are perpetually within effortless reach.

> *Pro Tip: Elevate your browsing experience by adroitly managing tabs through Safari's tab groups or by strategically bookmarking frequently visited websites. These practices pave the way for a clutter-free and organized virtual exploration.*

Private browsing mode and when to use it

Privacy, a cherished aspect of the digital age, beckons the utilization of Safari's private browsing mode.

This feature is instrumental when you seek to navigate the web incognito, leaving no trace within your browsing history.

Discerning when and why to engage this mode is pivotal for safeguarding your online confidentiality.

> *Pro Tip: Invoke the cloak of private browsing mode judiciously, particularly when venturing into the realms of gift shopping or researching sensitive subjects. This tactical maneuver ensures that cookies and browsing history remain unscathed.*

Block pop-ups and manage site settings

The intrusion of pop-up elements can be disruptive, diminishing the quality of your browsing experience. Safari extends to you the capacity to manage these unwelcome interferences via a pop-up blocker. Mastery over site settings further empowers you to customize your browsing experience by enabling or disabling features such as location access and notifications. This level of control ensures that websites align with your preferences.

Pro Tip: Exert fine-grained control over your browsing environment by wielding the ability to block pop-ups and customize site settings. These measures empower you to safeguard your privacy and security while traversing the digital landscape.

Tips to recognize safe sites and potential threats

Online safety stands as an omnipresent concern. Familiarity with techniques for identifying secure websites and recognizing potential hazards is indispensable. **The presence of "HTTPS" within the URL and a padlock icon in the address bar signify a secure connection.** Exercise vigilance when downloading files or inputting sensitive data on unfamiliar websites to ensure the protection of your digital domain.

Pro Tip: Sharpen your discerning eye when distinguishing digital safe havens from potential threats. Keep a vigilant lookout for the HTTPS protocol and the padlock icon in the address bar, be circumspect of domains sporting misspellings or dubious URLs.

Use complex passwords and manage passwords

Passwords, the sentinels of your digital realm, are artfully constructed and preserved within Safari. The browser can generate intricate, unique passwords, securely storing them in your iCloud Keychain. Unveil the art of leveraging this feature to augment your online security, thereby safeguarding your accounts against illicit access.

Pro Tip: Embark on the path to fortified digital fortresses by embracing the services of a trusted password manager, instrumental in the creation and secure storage of robust, idiosyncratic passwords for each online bastion. Safari extends a helping hand by proffering suggestions for intricate passwords.

Install Safari Extensions and how it works

Safari Extensions, akin to magical implements, possess the capacity to elevate your browsing experience. Mastery over the process of installing extensions from the App Store enables you to delve into a vast repository of functionalities. These add-ons encompass ad blockers, password managers, and an array of additional tools. Embark on a journey to explore the multitude of ways in which these extensions can optimize your online endeavors and fortify your digital security.

Pro Tip: Expand your digital horizons by augmenting your browsing experience with the incorporation of Safari Extensions. However, exercise due diligence by solely enlisting extensions emanating from reputable sources, and periodically prune your extensions roster to maintain optimal browsing efficiency and security.

7.2 Email

Configure the Mail app and add email accounts

The Mail app, a digital post office, bridges your connection to the digital world by accommodating email accounts from diverse providers. Proficiency in configuring the Mail app and adeptly incorporating and managing your email accounts guarantees uninterrupted connectivity, even while on the go.

Pro Tip: Navigate the labyrinth of email notifications with finesse by crafting customized notification settings for each email account within the Settings app, thereby circumventing the deluge of incessant interruptions.

Organize and manage emails: folders, flags, and archiving

A methodical approach to your inbox enhances productivity. The creation of folders for message categorization, flagging important emails for swift reference, and archiving correspondence, which is worth preservation but not immediate attention, render your digital communication organized and readily accessible.

NEW EMAIL

Pro Tip: Master the art of email governance by implementing discerning filters and rules that diligently presort incoming emails into designated folders, an indispensable tactic for maintaining inbox equilibrium.

Write, reply to, and forward emails

Email composition, response, and forwarding encompasses multifaceted intricacies. **Initiating the process involves accessing the "Compose" or "New Email"** interface and meticulously curating recipients while crafting an enticing subject line that encapsulates the email's essence.

The body of the email serves as the canvas for your message, requiring clarity, coherence, and brevity, with each paragraph advancing the narrative seamlessly.

Adding attachments, an integral aspect of modern communication, enhances the depth of your discourse, demanding discernment in file selection, format, and size. Security measures, including malware screening, ensure the safe transmission of attachments.

Upon dispatch, attachments become accessible to recipients through icons or hyperlinks, requiring vigilance in opening files from unverified sources. This comprehensive understanding of email intricacies empowers efficient and secure digital communication.

ADD ATTACHMENTS

SELECT ATTACHMENT TYPE

Pro Tip: Infuse your digital missives with a personalized touch by tailoring your email signature to encompass vital contact information, bestowing upon recipients the convenience of expedient communication.

Attachments: how to send and receive them safely

The fundamental competencies of crafting, responding to, and forwarding emails are elemental. Dive into the intricacies of skillfully composing emails, complete with attachments. Acquaint yourself with the nuances of sending and receiving attachments safely, streamlining your digital correspondence.

Pro Tip: Tread the path of caution when navigating the terrain of email attachments. Prior to opening these digital parcels, embark on a fact-finding mission to ascertain the sender's authenticity and scrutinize file types with a discerning eye, thereby ensuring a secure passage through the perilous waters of digital attachments.

Recognize suspicious emails and phishing

Phishing endeavors and dubious emails lurk as concealed threats in the digital expanse. Equip yourself with the discernment required to identify prevalent signs of fraudulent emails and phishing schemes. Profound comprehension of handling unsolicited or questionable emails bolsters your digital defenses.

Pro Tip: Set sail upon the tempestuous seas of email with a cautious demeanor. Exercise due diligence by hovering your cursor over links or employing a tap-and-hold strategy for mobile devices to unveil the veritable URLs prior to embarking on hyperlink journeys. Vigilance is paramount when perusing emails soliciting sensitive information.

How to behave when faced with unsolicited or suspicious emails

When confronted with unsolicited or dubious emails, the ability to discern appropriate courses of action is indispensable. This section provides guidance on the judicious responses that should be employed, thereby fortifying your digital persona and personal data.

Pro Tip: When besieged by the unbidden, exercise prudence by relegating unsolicited emails from unfamiliar senders to the annals of deletion, without partaking in the opening of enigmatic attachments or traversing obscure links.

Enable and use two-factor authentication

Two-factor authentication (2FA) emerges as a formidable bastion in the realm of digital security. Discover the processes of enabling and deploying 2FA for your email accounts, **introducing an additional layer of safeguarding for your digital presence.** With 2FA, the authentication process extends beyond the confines of a mere password, rendering unauthorized access nearly insurmountable.

Pro Tip: Fortify the citadel of your email accounts by instating the sentinel known as two-factor authentication (2FA). This added security layer deters would-be intruders by demanding secondary verification, thereby safeguarding your epistolary treasures.

7.3 Apple Pay for Online Payments

What is Apple Pay and how it works

Apple Pay serves as your conduit to frictionless and secure online as well as in-store transactions. Delve into the intricacies of this digital wallet, starting with the configuration process and the inclusion of your payment cards.

Unearth the methodology for effecting online and in-store purchases via Apple Pay, thereby unlocking a realm of convenience while ensuring the inviolability of your financial data.

> *Pro Tip: Embark on an odyssey of comprehension by unraveling the intricacies of Apple Pay, a digital symphony harmonizing secure transactions across a myriad of locations and apps.*

Configure Apple Pay and add cards

The bedrock of Apple Pay lies in the seamless amalgamation of your payment cards. Comprehend the steps involved in configuring Apple Pay, which entails the inclusion of your credit or debit cards within your digital wallet. This straightforward process sets the stage for secure transactions in both virtual and physical realms.

> *Pro Tip: Maintain the course of seamless and secure transactions by deftly configuring Apple Pay and diligently overseeing the addition and removal of cards. Regular scrutiny and purging of archaic or disused cards is a cardinal practice.*

Make online and in-store purchases with Apple Pay

Wallet

Once your payment cards repose securely within Apple Pay, explore the seamlessness inherent in conducting transactions, whether in the digital or tangible sphere. Ascertain the procedures for initiating payments through a simple tap or click, whether your shopping escapades lead you to favored e-commerce platforms or brick-and-mortar establishments. These functionalities proffer not only convenience but also robust protective measures, safeguarding the sanctity of your financial information during every transaction.

> *Pro Tip: Navigate the labyrinthine terrain of online and in-store transactions with aplomb. In physical brick-and-mortar establishments, expedite the process by a mere double-click of the side button on your device, a quicker and more convenient alternative to fumbling for an app.*

Security and privacy with Apple Pay: why it's safe

Unravel the strata of security and privacy enveloping Apple Pay. Gain insights into the rationale behind its status as a dependable choice for your digital wallet. Acquaint yourself with transaction monitoring and the resolution of common issues, thereby ensuring the imperviousness of your financial data.

Pro Tip: Safeguard your monetary sanctum with regular vigilance. The scrutiny of your Apple Pay transaction history serves as a formidable bulwark, swiftly detecting any intrusions or anomalies in your financial domain.

View and manage transactions with Apple Pay

Apple Pay fosters transparency in the realm of financial transactions. Master the procedures for monitoring and overseeing your transactions, which enable you to maintain a vigilant eye on the activity of your digital wallet.

Pro Tip: Uncover the gamut of transaction dynamics governing Apple Pay, ranging from the thresholds of purchase limits to the multifaceted realm of authentication methods.

Troubleshoot common Apple Pay issues

Like any technological innovation, Apple Pay may occasionally encounter hitches. Equip yourself with the knowledge and techniques for resolving prevalent predicaments, thus facilitating the seamless functionality of your digital wallet.

Pro Tip: In the labyrinth of Apple Pay conundrums, such as the vexing specter of declined transactions, maintain your equilibrium. Scrutinize the status of your card, and, if necessity dictates, establish communication with your financial institution for timely resolution.

Additional tips for online security

In the realm of online security, maintaining a vigilant stance remains of utmost significance. Assure the presence of robust, distinct passcodes for the entirety of your online accounts, contemplate the activation of two-factor authentication wherever it is made available, and exercise prudence when disseminating personal or financial information through virtual channels. Routinely update your software and applications to rectify potential security vulnerabilities, and acquaint yourself with the latest developments in cyber threats and stratagems of phishing. Lastly, employ esteemed security software and fortified firewalls to reinforce the protective bastions of your digital citadel.

Pro Tip: A comprehensive approach to the domain of online security necessitates perpetual erudition, preemptive actions, and an acute cognizance of the nascent perils that may emerge. Remain abreast of developments and adapt your online methodologies accordingly, assuring the safeguarding of your digital presence.

Chapter 8:

8.1 "Health" App and data tracking

Overview of the Health app: interface and main categories

The "Health" application serves as a versatile instrument, functioning as a central nexus for the oversight and governance of an array of health-related facets.

Health

Upon initiation, the user is presented with an uncluttered and user-friendly interface, which categorizes health-centric data into distinct sections like "Summary," "All Health Data," and "Medical ID."

Each category fulfills a distinct role in assisting individuals in conducting a thorough evaluation of their well-being.

"Summary" extends an expansive selection of health and fitness subjects for exploration, proffering valuable insights and information.

"All Health Data" serves as the repository for an individual's

personal health data, meticulously arranging vital statistics such as weight, height, and blood pressure, alongside fitness-related metrics including step counts and sleep analysis.

Finally, **"Medical ID"** provides the capability to include crucial medical information and contact details for emergencies, ensuring that vital data is promptly accessible in times of need. This well-structured interface empowers users to navigate their health journey with consummate ease..

> *Pro Tip: Tailor your Health app dashboard to your preferences, ensuring that it showcases the health metrics and data categories most pertinent to your well-being goals.*

How to manually enter health data (e.g. weight, height, blood pressure)

The "Health" application presents users with the flexibility to manually input imperative health data, affording individuals the capacity to maintain an exhaustive record of their well-being.

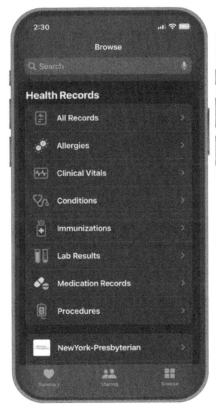
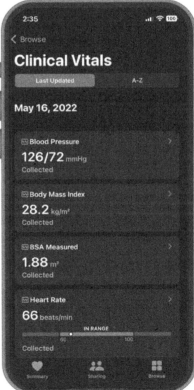

Whether one intends to monitor fluctuations in weight, document height alterations, or track blood pressure readings, this application streamlines the process with utmost efficacy.

The accuracy of data input is of paramount importance, as it substantiates that the insights and trends generated by the application are both meaningful and precise.

By comprehending the process of manually entering data, users attain heightened control over the health metrics they scrutinize, contributing to a more comprehensive overview of their health expedition.

Pro Tip: Consistency is key when it comes to manually inputting health data. Keep your records up to date for precise insights, especially regarding vital metrics such as weight, height, and blood pressure.

Automatic tracking:

Step count, sleep cycle, and physical activity

In the pursuit of a healthier lifestyle, the meticulous monitoring of daily activities assumes paramount importance.

In this regard, the "Health" application excels, capitalizing on its automated tracking capabilities. It seamlessly records metrics such as step counts, diligently monitors sleep cycles, and evaluates levels of physical activity.

For individuals who aspire to maintain an active lifestyle while nurturing equilibrium in their daily routines, this attribute proves invaluable.

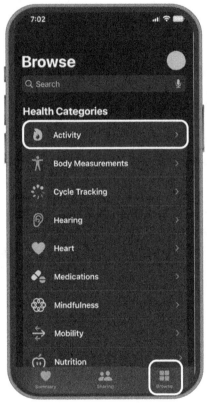 

The application operates surreptitiously in the background, perpetually supplying insights into daily routines devoid of the exigency for ceaseless manual inputs. It is a tool thoughtfully conceived to streamline the process of health vigilance.

Pro Tip: Harness the potential of automated data tracking by having your iPhone accompany you during physical activities. The integrated motion sensors play a pivotal role in ensuring accurate step counts and sleep cycle monitoring.

View trends and analyze data

Nested within the confines of the "Health" application is a repository of data that spans across days, weeks, months, and even years. This extensive reservoir of information enables users to trace health trends and conduct comprehensive well-being assessments.

Visual depictions such as charts and graphs furnish lucid portrayals of progress over time, empowering individuals to discern patterns and render informed determinations regarding their health. Whether the endeavor involves monitoring weight fluctuations, scrutinizing sleep quality, or gauging physical activity levels, the capacity to scrutinize data and identify trends bequeaths valuable insights into the trajectory of one's health voyage.

> *Pro Tip: Dive deep into the data trends and analytical tools provided by the Health app. This wealth of information allows you to discern patterns and make well-informed decisions regarding your health and fitness goals.*

Share health data with doctors or other apps

The "Health" application upholds a stringent commitment to data privacy and confidentiality while affording a secure avenue for the dissemination of health data to healthcare professionals or compatible applications. This functionality ensures that one's invaluable health information can be harnessed to enhance well-being.

The process transpires seamlessly, aligning harmoniously with the broader healthcare milieu, nurturing collaboration and fostering well-informed decision-making.

Of noteworthy significance, robust data privacy measures stand resolutely in place to safeguard sensitive health information, affording users a sense of serenity as they divulge their data to trusted entities.

> *Pro Tip: When sharing your health data, whether with healthcare professionals or other applications, exercise discretion by perusing and customizing the privacy settings. Grant access solely to reputable sources and relevant parties.*

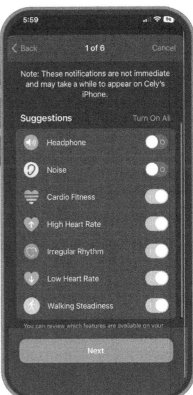

Data privacy: how Apple protects your health information

The fortification of privacy stands as a pivotal facet in the stewardship of health data. In the contemporary digital epoch, the preservation of sensitive health information assumes paramount importance. The "Health" application stands as a bastion of data privacy and security, predicated upon Apple's unwavering dedication to the cause.

Users can repose unwavering trust in the conscientious management of their health data, assured that it is handled with the utmost circumspection and protection. This section expounds upon the resolute measures undertaken by Apple, delineating the encryption protocols, user consent prerequisites, and data governance features that, in concert, conspire to engender a secure environment for health oversight.

> *Pro Tip: Familiarize yourself with Apple's robust data privacy measures within the Health app. Your health information is cocooned in layers of encryption and authentication, ensuring that your confidentiality remains sacrosanct.*

Add emergency contacts in the Health app

Emergencies can transpire precipitously, underscoring the significance of having pivotal information readily accessible. The "Health" application confers upon users the prerogative to seamlessly incorporate emergency contacts.

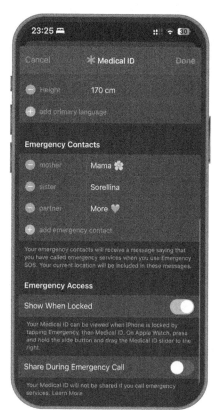

These contacts serve as a lifeline during critical junctures, ensuring that germane data can be expeditiously accessed when it matters most. This feature elevates preparedness to a heightened echelon, permitting users to input essential particulars concerning their emergency contacts, including the nature of their relationship and contact information.

In moments of exigency, such as medical crises, this information can be promptly retrieved, potentially conferring life-saving advantages. The capacity to include emergency contacts exemplifies a proactive measure in the prioritization of safety and well-being.

> *Pro Tip: Within the Health app, meticulously input emergency contact details, including names, relationships, and phone numbers. This data assumes paramount importance during unforeseen medical emergencies.*

8.2 Importance of emergency contacts and how they can be used

How to add, edit, or remove emergency contacts

Emergency contacts, often unsung heroes in moments of crisis, necessitate adept management. Acquainting oneself with the procedure for integrating, altering, or erasing these contacts within the iPhone is imperative. This section provides comprehensive directives on the intricacies of effectually administrating emergency contacts. It elucidates the methodology for appending new contacts, revising extant entries, and expunging outdated information. Proficiency in these tasks warrants that one's roster of emergency contacts remains current and efficaciously serves its pivotal role in ensuring safety and well-being.

> *Pro Tip: To guarantee the efficacy of your emergency contacts, periodically review and update this roster. Ensure it remains an accurate reflection of your current relationships and contact information.*

Use the emergency SOS function and automatically notify emergency contacts

The Emergency SOS function assumes a position of paramount significance in the realm of iPhone safety.

It transcends the role of mere location identification for misplaced devices, constituting a comprehensive safety feature that, when harnessed effectively, can be a lifeline during dire circumstances.

This section delves into the intricacies of the Emergency SOS function, furnishing step-by-step instructions on how to leverage it to optimal effect.

Beyond its capacity to summon emergency services, this feature undertakes the automatic notification of pre-designated

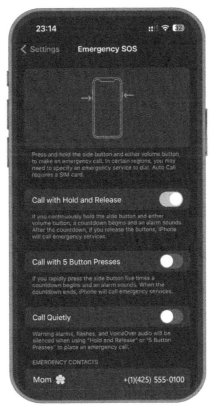
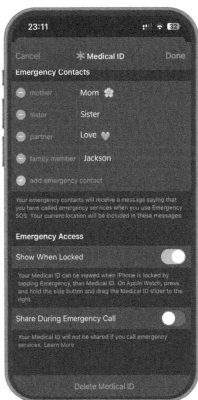

emergency contacts. It serves as a safety net that can prove instrumental in urgent scenarios, and a grasp of its operative intricacies can substantially enhance safeguarding one's well-being.

Pro Tip: Delve into the workings of the Emergency SOS feature on your iPhone. Mastery of its activation can be pivotal in swiftly responding to urgent situations.

Create a medical card that can be viewed from the lock screen

In times of emergency, every moment is consequential.

One of the salient attributes of the iPhone is its capacity to generate a Medical ID card that can be promptly viewed from the lock screen.

This card encompasses vital health information, including allergies, medical conditions, and emergency contact particulars.

Within this section, users will gain proficiency in establishing and customizing their Medical ID cards, thereby ensuring that pivotal information is accessible to first responders when exigency strikes.

This constitutes a proactive measure that elevates safety and expedites the provision of crucial data during emergencies.

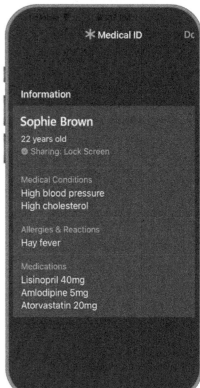

Pro Tip: Maximize the utility of your Medical ID card by furnishing it with comprehensive medical information, encompassing allergies, blood type, and existing medical conditions. This card is readily accessible from your lock screen, furnishing vital details to first responders.

8.3 Enable "Find My iPhone" for additional security

Find My

Overview and importance of "Find My iPhone"

"Find My iPhone" transcends the realm of a mere tool for tracking misplaced devices.

It embodies a comprehensive security feature that superimposes an additional stratum of safeguarding upon one's iPhone. This section introduces users to the import and multifarious ways in which "Find My iPhone" amplifies the security parameters of their device.

Whether one's iPhone has been lost or pilfered, a comprehensive understanding of this feature's capabilities is imperative.

> *Pro Tip: To fortify your security framework comprehensively, integrate all your Apple devices into the "Find My iPhone" service. This umbrella of protection extends to iPhones, iPads, Macs, and even AirPods.*

Configure and activate the service

To harness the capabilities conferred by "Find My iPhone," the initial undertaking necessitates the configuration and activation of this service.

This section elucidates the steps involved in this preparatory process, ensuring that one's device is poised to derive maximum benefits from this security feature. It encompasses indispensable procedures, including the activation of location services and the meticulous verification of Apple ID settings.

> *Pro Tip: Seamlessly set up "Find My iPhone" during your device's initial configuration or within the iCloud settings. Activate location services to ensure your device remains traceable in the event of loss.*

How to use "Find My iPhone" to locate a lost device

The disheartening experience of misplacing an iPhone can engender considerable duress. However, with "Find My iPhone" at one's disposal, an efficacious resolution is within reach. This section furnishes exhaustive guidelines on how to effectually employ this feature to pinpoint the precise location of a lost device.

Whether the device has been ensconced within the recesses of upholstery or mislaid in a public domain, "Find My iPhone" can expedite its recovery.

> *Pro Tip: In the unfortunate scenario of a misplaced device, utilize the "Find My" app on another Apple device or access the iCloud website for pinpoint location, sound playback, or remote device locking functionalities.*

Lost mode: how it works and how it protects your data

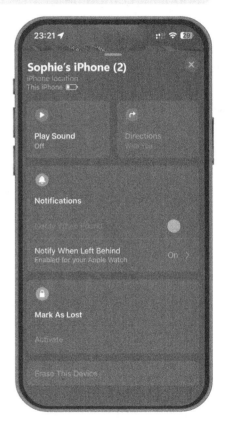

In circumstances wherein an iPhone has gone astray, the activation of Lost Mode can metamorphose the situation. This section expounds upon the mechanics of Lost Mode and delves into the facets of data security that it enhances.

Beyond the location identification, Lost Mode empowers the user to remotely immobilize the device and display a customized message incorporating contact information. This ensues that if a benevolent individual encounters the misplaced device, they can facilitate its return.

> *Pro Tip: Should your device go astray, invoke Lost Mode as a strategic response. This feature not only secures your device but also displays a custom message and contact information on the lock screen.*

Remote deletion: how and when to use it

In certain scenarios, the sanctity of data assumes preeminence. Remote data deletion is a potent tool for safeguarding information in the event of a stolen or lost iPhone. This section affords insight into the mechanics of remote data deletion, accompanied by delineations of the circumstances under which the invocation of this feature is judicious. It emerges as a pre-emptive measure that forestalls unauthorized access to one's data in scenarios marked by theft or loss.

> *Pro Tip: In cases where sensitive data is at stake, consider remote data erasure as a last resort. This proactive measure wipes all data from the lost device, safeguarding your privacy.*

8.4 Reminders to take medication or medical appointments

Enable fall detection on the Apple Watch (if owned)

The Apple Watch transcends the ambit of a mere fashionable accessory; it can emerge as a lifeline in moments of crisis. **Fall detection stands as a feature that can autonomously identify falls and extend assistance as necessary.** In this section, users will discover the steps requisite for enabling fall detection on their Apple Watch, contingent on ownership. This feature assumes heightened significance for wearers, particularly those susceptible to falls.

> *Pro Tip: Apple Watch users can reinforce their safety net by enabling fall detection within the Watch app on their iPhones. This feature can automatically summon emergency services upon detecting a significant fall.*

Use the noise measurement function to protect your hearing

Hearing health serves as a pivotal component of overall well-being. The noise measurement function integrated into the iPhone assumes the role of a custodian for hearing health. It issues alerts pertaining to potentially injurious noise levels in the user's surroundings, affording the opportunity for requisite precaution. This section expounds upon the process of enabling and efficaciously utilizing this function, ensuring that individuals adopt a proactive stance in preserving their auditory well-being.

> *Pro Tip: Safeguard your auditory health by vigilantly monitoring noise levels through the noise measurement function on your Apple Watch. Adjust your surroundings or employ hearing protection when exposed to elevated noise levels.*

Set up and use local emergency notifications

Remaining apprised of safety advisories within one's vicinity assumes primordial importance. Local emergency notifications furnish critical information during emergencies or natural calamities. This section offers comprehensive guidance on the process of configuring and utilizing local emergency notifications, guaranteeing the prompt receipt of time-sensitive alerts that can prove decisive in safeguarding one's safety.

Be it severe meteorological alerts or other local exigencies, preparedness constitutes the linchpPro Tip: Apple Watch users can reinforce their safety net by enabling fall detection within the Watch app on their iPhones. This feature can automatically summon emergency services upon detecting a significant fall in in ensuring well-being.

> *Pro Tip: Enhance your preparedness by acquainting yourself with local emergency notification settings on your iPhone. These notifications offer crucial information during emergencies, helping you stay vigilant and secure.*

This enriched content chapter augments the depth of knowledge and proficiency attainable concerning the "Health" app, emergency contacts, "Find My iPhone" security, and medical reminders on your iPhone.

Chapter 9:

9.1 Calendar

Create and Manage Events

Calendar

The **Calendar application** on your iPhone proves itself as a multifaceted **instrument for the meticulous orchestration of your timetable. Events materialize at your fingertips with a mere tap on the "+" icon,** granting you the ability to input event particulars such as nomenclature, date, temporal allocations, and rendezvous locale.

This uncomplicated procedure bestows utmost convenience in appending appointments, rendezvous, or any form of commitments into your schedule. Furthermore, **it offers the prospect of establishing recurrent events for activities that cyclically ensue, such as weekly assemblies or monthly commemorative occasions.**

This particular facet emerges as especially beneficial for individuals ensnared by repetitive obligations, thus sparing them

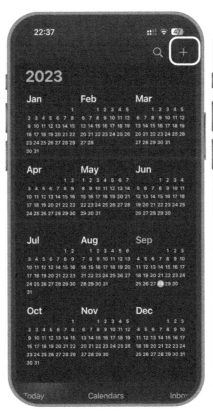

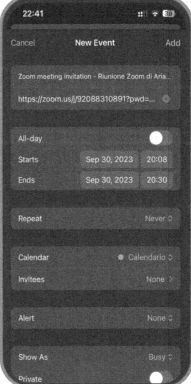

the tedium of recurrent data entry. Administering events is an effortless undertaking; you wield the power to modify, obliterate, or reschedule them as exigencies demand, thereby ensuring that your calendar remains a perennially current and adaptive entity harmonized with the evolving cadence of your life.

> *Pro Tip: Employ color-coded calendars for the visual differentiation of personal, work-related, and familial events, facilitating streamlined schedule management at a glance.*

Add birthdays and holidays

The conundrum of commemorating birthdays and holidays metamorphoses into an elementary task thanks to the Calendar app. The ability to seamlessly infuse the birthdays of your contacts into the app ushers forth an automated system of anticipatory reminders.

This ingenious facet serves as a bulwark against the ignominy of neglecting a cherished individual's natal celebration, affording you the luxury of preemptive preparations for festive observances. Furthermore, the app's dexterity extends to the display of national and regional holidays contingent upon your geographic location.

This feature fosters a state of perennial enlightenment concerning significant calendar milestones devoid of any manual intervention. Irrespective of whether your peregrinations bear you to foreign climes or confine you to familiar precincts, the Calendar app remains a steadfast sentinel, guaranteeing that you remain cognizant of public holidays. This, in turn, expedites the process of structuring your activities and leisure in synchrony with the dictates of the calendar.

> *Pro Tip: Synchronize your contacts with the Calendar app to enable the automatic population of birthdays, and subscribe to holiday calendars for up-to-date information on upcoming festivities.*

Set alarms and notifications for events

The imperative of never allowing an important event to elude your awareness crystallizes into reality through the facility to establish alarms and notifications for your calendar-based occurrences. **This functionality bestows upon you the prerogative to receive timely reminders calibrated in consonance with your predilections.**

Whether your penchant leans toward a perfunctory alert or a more elaborate notification furnished with advanced forewarning, the Calendar app adjusts itself to your idiosyncratic exigencies. Consequently, you retain the autonomy to dictate the temporal interval that precedes an event's commencement, a facet of particular utility in scenarios where preparatory endeavors span multiple phases or necessitate a protracted traverse to the event's venue.

With this pliable notification framework, the Calendar app metamorphoses into more than a mere repository of records; it transmutes into a proactive aide, adeptly shepherding you in the endeavor of maintaining strict adherence to your timetable.

Pro Tip: Tailor event notifications to your preferences by adjusting lead times, ensuring adequate preparation for each appointment or meeting.

Share calendars with family and friends

The cultivation of collaborative undertakings assumes an effortless character via the faculty of calendar sharing. Whether the ambit entails familial rendezvous or professional rendezvous, the act of calendar-sharing with family members, associates, or workmates streamlines the process of information interchange and calendrical coordination.

This section facilitates a navigational sojourn elucidating the paradigm of calendar-sharing, encompassing the apportionment of view-only or edit-permitted access rights and the efficient administration of shared calendars. The landscape of sharing is marked by its flexibility, accommodating a gamut of access control levels, thus ensuring that you can safeguard your privacy when the need arises, while concurrently promoting a milieu conducive to open collaboration.

By harnessing the capacity of shared calendars, you partake in a harmonious synchronization of your plans with others, thereby engendering a synergistic dynamic that forestalls the encumbrance of scheduling clashes. In summation, the Calendar app embodies more than the persona of a mere personal schedular tool; it metamorphoses into a versatile implement for the propagation of organizational acumen and the fostering of unbroken links with your social and vocational circles.

Pro Tip: Foster collaboration and coordination by selectively sharing specific calendars with family members or colleagues, wielding control over who possesses viewing and editing privileges within the settings.

9.2 Reminders

Create, edit, and delete reminders

The Reminders application stands as a potent instrument for orchestrating assignments and cataloging to-do lists. This segment delves into the art of initiating, adapting, and abolishing task prompts with effortless finesse. You shall acquire the skills to imbue your reminders with attributes such as priority ratings, due dates, and supplementary annotations, thereby ensuring a systematic and efficient approach to task administration.

Task initiation is as straightforward as the input of textual information, yet the application grants you advanced capabilities like the allocation of deadlines and the gradation of importance, affording a comprehensive scheme for effective task organization.

Reminders

The processes of task modification and eradication are equally uncomplicated, affording the flexibility to refine your roster of duties as your priorities evolve. The facility to annex notes to your task prompts endows them with additional context and minutiae, facilitating the expeditious fulfillment of assignments.

Pro Tip: Enhance task prioritization by assigning due dates and times to your reminders, enabling a sharper focus on immediate tasks.

Set location-based reminders

The advent of location-cognizant task reminders heralds a paradigm shift in the management of location-dependent tasks. Whether it entails a prompt to procure provisions when in proximity to the store or a memorandum to collect dry cleaning on your homeward-bound trajectory, this feature ensconces you in the realm of forget-me-not efficiency.

This segment delineates an elucidative path towards the configuration and utilization of location-aware reminders. **By harnessing the GPS capabilities inherent in your iPhone, the Reminders app assumes the mantle of a sentinel.** It dispatches notifications upon your ingress into or egress from pre-defined geographic coordinates, culminating in a seamless integration of locale-specific tasks into your quotidian routines. The transformative prowess of this feature augments your productivity by interweaving tasks with your daily perambulations.

Pro Tip: Harness the power of location-based reminders to receive alerts upon arriving at or departing from designated places, such as the grocery store or your workplace.

Organize reminders into lists

The faculty to systematize your task prompts into catalogs constitutes a pivotal facet of the Reminders app. This segment underscores the advantages of resorting to catalogs for the taxonomy of your assignments and extends guidance on their initiation, adaptation, and administration.

The arrangement of tasks into catalogs engenders an organized and methodical approach to task completion. It endows you with the prerogative to spawn discrete catalogs catering to distinct spheres of endeavor, be it occupational commitments, personal errands, or more. By virtue of this stratagem, your tasks remain methodically compartmentalized and readily accessible. Additionally, the utilization of catalogs bequeaths a seamless avenue for collaboration, facilitating

the sharing of particular catalogs with other individuals. Whether it encompasses a familial shopping inventory or a project task ledger in a professional milieu, the deployment of catalogs assumes paramount import. Employed efficaciously, the Reminders app materializes as a versatile implement for the management of tasks of variegated natures and complexities.

Share reminder lists with others

The spirit of collaborative undertakings pervades the domain of task reminders. The potential to bestow access to your task prompt catalogs upon family members, comrades, or associates heralds an era of communal task management.

This segment elucidates the procedural intricacies of endowing access to task prompt catalogs, stipulating access rights, and collaborating harmoniously on task-related endeavors. This facet unfurls a panorama of real-time updates and harmonization among multiple participants, ensconcing a state of perpetual synchronization. Whether the undertaking pertains to event planning, household chores, or professional project endeavors, the abutment of task prompt catalogs engenders a climate of collective endeavor and heightened efficiency.

This collaborative dimension of the Reminders app magnifies its profile into a flexible instrument for task administration on both individual and collective levels, accentuating efficiency and organization across diverse facets of existence.

9.3 Notes

Create, edit, and delete notes

Notes

The Notes application stands as the digital equivalent of your trusty notepad, and this section elucidates the rudiments of generating, modifying, and erasing notes. Whether you're transcribing brainwaves, composing to-do inventories, or preserving critical facts within arm's reach, the Notes app proffers an effortless conduit.

The inception of a note is as facile as inaugurating the app and applying the "+" icon. After the commencement of a note, you can effortlessly tinker with its contents, format, and arrangement.

This capability shines when revisiting and augmenting your notes subsequently. Should you ascertain a note redundant, the app permits its deletion with equal simplicity.

These foundational actions of engendering, amending, and obliterating notes underpin your digital note-taking odyssey, assuring a capacity to capture and administer information efficaciously.

Pro Tip: Elevate your note-taking game by introducing organizational paradigms such as folders or categories, ensuring the cohesion of similar notes and facilitating efficient retrieval.

Use formatting and checklists in notes

Notes transcend the realm of mere text; they lend themselves to formatting and systematization. This segment plunges into the repertoire of formatting choices at your disposal within the Notes app, spanning headers, bullet points, and enumeration.

Furthermore, it probes the realm of fashioning and monitoring checklists inside your notes, endowing the app with impressive task management capabilities. With the prowess to format your notes, you assume the mantle of a craftsman, fashioning structured and visually pleasing documents wherein pivotal data commands the spotlight.

The checklist functionality elevates task management to an entirely new echelon, facilitating the creation of to-do enumerations inside your notes. This trait confers the ability to tick off accomplished tasks and oversee your headway. Whether it entails organizing your musings or orchestrating ventures, the formatting and checklist characteristics encapsulated within the Notes app enrich your note-taking panache.

Pro Tip: Exploit the panoply of formatting tools encompassing headings, bullet points, and numbered lists to delineate the structure of your notes. Furthermore, imbue your notes with task management capabilities by incorporating checkboxes within to-do lists.

Share notes and collaborate in real-time

The theater of collaboration assumes center stage, ushered in by the capacity to share notes and embark on concurrent editing ventures with peers.

This segment steers you through the act of note dissemination, the extension of invitations to collaborators, and the hallowed domain of real-time co-editing. It's a feature that augments efficiency and teamwork. The act of sharing notes transpires with effortless ease via a sequence of taps, inviting others to peruse or embellish your notes.

This cooperative vista fosters productive group dynamics, be it brainstorming ideas, framing meeting agendas, or collaborating on academic assignments. The concept of real-time editing assures that every participant remains synchronized with the most recent changes, negating the necessity for ceaseless communication pertaining to document updates. The ability to collaborate harmoniously within the Notes app engenders it into a pliable instrument catering to both individual and professional requisites, thereby amplifying efficiency and expediting information exchange.

Pro Tip: Foster collaborative endeavors by enabling real-time editing and sharing of notes, a potent tool for collectively curating shopping lists or orchestrating project blueprints.

Lock notes with password or Face ID/Touch ID

In the domain of personal notes, privacy reigns supreme. The Notes app affords you the opportunity to safeguard specific notes through the imposition of a password or the authentication bestowed by Face ID or Touch ID, upholding the tenets of enhanced security.

This section expounds upon the methodologies to shield your sensitive data ensconced within notes, thereby safeguarding the sanctity of your private ruminations and confidential data. The act of securing notes bequeaths an additional stratum of defense to your digital repository. Be it the preservation of personal reflections, crucial access codes, or confidential records, this trait ensures that your notes are immune to unsanctioned access.

The choice between a password or the biometric elegance of Face ID or Touch ID renders it a user-friendly yet highly fortified shield. The jurisdiction over privacy thus ascertained verifies that the Notes app functions not just as an authoritative note-taking instrument, but also as a secure vault for your confidential data.

Pro Tip: Shore up the defenses of sensitive information by fortifying notes with passwords or the impenetrable bulwark of biometric authentication, thus ensconcing your privacy, even in scenarios where others gain access to your device.

9.4 Music

Overview of the Music app: library, search, and playback

Music

The Music app serves as your portal to an extensive realm of auditory amusement. This section furnishes a comprehensive insight into the app's user interface, encompassing the art of navigating your music repository, conducting in-depth song searches, and instigating playback.

Upon initiation of the Music app, your music collection unveils itself in an organized manner, featuring distinct segments for songs, albums, artists, and playlists. Navigation through your assemblage becomes a seamless affair, facilitated by intuitive swipes and taps, allowing for the effortless unearthing of the desired musical selection.

The search functionality stands as a potent instrument, affording the rapid pinpointing of particular songs, albums, or artists within your expansive inventory. Once the optimal track is located, the act of commencing playback is as elementary as a mere tap. This all-encompassing guide ensures your adeptness in traversing your music compendium and savoring your preferred melodies with consummate ease.

Pro Tip: Elevate your music-listening experience by crafting mood or activity-based playlists, akin to curating bespoke radio stations tailored to your preferences.

Purchase and download music from the App Store

For devotees of music, the capacity to purchase and download songs directly from the App Store represents an invaluable facet. This segment elucidates the procedural steps for the acquisition of cherished tunes, enabling the creation of a bespoke music compilation.

The acquisition of music entails a visit to the App Store, where a quest for favored tracks culminates in a secure transaction. Upon download, these songs become seamlessly assimilated into your Music app library.

This feature proves to be of exceptional utility for the discovery of new music or the procurement of specific compositions destined for perpetual retention. It offers a convenient mechanism for the expansion of your musical anthology, guaranteeing unfettered access to your preferred harmonies, irrespective of connectivity status.

> *Pro Tip: Append music selections to your wishlist within the App Store, vigilantly awaiting opportune discounts or promotions that enable cost-effective expansion of your music library.*

Create and manage personalized playlists

The crafting of personalized playlists emerges as an exceptional strategy for the curation of your auditory journey.

Whether the objective is to set a tranquil ambiance with a mellifluous compilation or to imbue vivacity into a workout regimen via an invigorating mix, this segment expounds on the facile construction and governance of personalized playlists.

The assembly of these playlists entails the aggregation of songs from your library, their allocation of distinctive appellations, and the facultative reordering of track sequences, culminating in the cultivation of an idyllic listening expedition.

The administration of playlists retains a straightforward demeanor, permitting the addition or removal of songs in alignment with the mutability of musical predilections.

These personalized compilations bear a semblance to contemporary digital mixtapes, authorizing the harmonization of music with specific occasions or emotional states. Whether your proclivity leans toward casual auditions or ardent musical curation, this facet of the Music app elevates your enjoyment and emotional connection with cherished tunes.

Stream music with Apple Music (if available)

Apple Music stands as a subscription-based amenity, extending admittance to an expansive repertoire of songs. This section acquaints you with the art of navigating Apple Music, streaming melodies, generating custom playlists, and uncovering novel compositions. It constitutes essential reading for individuals seeking to fathom the Music app's complete spectrum of capabilities.

A subscription to Apple Music confers access to an almost boundless musical anthology, encompassing the latest releases and meticulously curated playlists. Within Apple Music's precincts, songs, albums, and artists are easily discoverable, with the option to append them to your library and formulate bespoke playlists.

The innate ability to unearth new music in consonance with your preferences serves as an exclusive feature, acquainting you with compositions you might otherwise remain unacquainted with. The act of music streaming via Apple Music engenders an immersive and dynamic auditory journey, transmogrifying your Music app into a conduit for the exploration and savored indulgence of a diversified universe of music.

9.5 Video

Watch videos and movies with the TV app or other streaming apps

TV

The TV app functions as the central hub for your video-based entertainment endeavors. Whether your viewing preferences lean towards movies, television series, or miscellaneous video content, this section embarks on a comprehensive exploration of how to efficiently navigate the TV app while accessing your preferred video content.

Additionally, it touches upon the utilization of alternative streaming applications to diversify your cinematic encounters. The TV app serves as a unifying nexus for your multifarious video-related requisites. It adeptly consolidates content from an assortment of sources, encompassing Apple TV+, iTunes, and third-party streaming services. This amalgamation of resources simplifies the process of discovering and indulging in your favored shows and movies.

Navigational elements such as category perusal, targeted title searches, and personalized viewing recommendations, based on your viewing history, amplify the user experience. Moreover, this section underscores the seamless integration of external streaming applications, permitting direct access to platforms such as Netflix, Hulu, or Disney+ from within the TV app. This holistic approach streamlines your entertainment choices, elevating the overall quality of your cinematic escapades.

> *Pro Tip: Navigate the realm of visual entertainment by harnessing the "Up Next" feature of the TV app, ensuring you never miss an episode of your favorite shows or movies.*

Purchase or rent movies from the App Store

The option to either purchase or rent movies directly through the App Store confers convenience and adaptability. This section delineates the step-by-step procedure for acquiring movies, tailored to meet your cinematic preferences, whether it be ephemeral viewing or the acquisition of enduring ownership.

The App Store's integration introduces the flexibility of renting or purchasing movies, thereby accommodating diverse preferences regarding the accessibility and longevity of preferred films. Renting is an ideal choice for one-time viewing, while acquisition results in the incorporation of the chosen film into your digital collection.

The expansive library features a diverse array of titles, each complemented by detailed descriptions and informative trailers to facilitate informed decision-making. Once the selection process concludes, the App Store's secure payment mechanism guarantees a streamlined transaction experience. This attribute furnishes instantaneous access to your chosen cinematic productions, enabling their enjoyment on your iPhone or facilitating their streaming onto other compatible devices via the AirPlay feature.

Pro Tip: Exercise patience and vigilance to seize special deals or discounts on cinematic treasures within the App Store, maximizing the entertainment value of your investments.

Use AirPlay to broadcast videos to other devices

AirPlay stands as a versatile attribute that empowers you to broadcast your iPhone's screen or content onto other compatible devices. This section elucidates the intricacies of utilizing AirPlay to relay videos to external devices, thereby facilitating a seamless and immersive viewing encounter on expansive screens.

AirPlay bestows upon your iPhone the capacity to function as a potent remote control, thereby facilitating the presentation of videos on devices that boast compatibility, such as Apple TV or smart TVs. Establishing a wireless connection between your iPhone and these apparatuses enables the effortless streaming of videos, photographs, or even the mirroring of your entire screen.

This functionality ushers in a realm of possibilities, from cinematic indulgence on a television screen to the presentation of business materials and the communal sharing of vacation snapshots with friends and family. The straightforwardness and versatility of AirPlay imbue it with inestimable worth as a

valuable addition to your arsenal of entertainment utilities, thus facilitating the enjoyment of content on more expansive canvases with consummate ease.

Pro Tip: Share the delight of your cherished videos with friends and family through the utilization of AirPlay, a seamless conduit for streaming content to compatible devices like Apple TV.

9.6 Brain Games

The importance of cognitive stimulation games for the elderly

Cognitive challenges have demonstrated their immense value in upholding mental acuity, especially within the older population. In this section, we delve into the profound importance of cognitive challenges in preserving cognitive faculties, memory retention, and overall psychological wellness.

We elucidate why these challenges hold profound significance for individuals across diverse age groups. Cognitive challenges, frequently referred to as brain challenges, encompass a spectrum of activities meticulously crafted to push the boundaries of cognitive functioning. Within the elderly demographic, the relevance of these challenges is particularly pronounced, as they serve as potent tools for mitigating cognitive degeneration and memory atrophy.

Consistent engagement with cognitive challenges has been empirically associated with enhancements in memory capacity, adeptness in problem-solving, and an elongated attention span. Furthermore, they serve as wellsprings of mental invigoration and recreation, an elemental component of holistic psychological welfare.

This section proffers insights into the scientific substantiation underscoring the merits of cognitive challenges while underscoring their pertinence across diverse age brackets, with a particular focus on seniors endeavoring to safeguard cognitive vitality.

Pro Tip: Infuse cognitive health into your daily routine by integrating brain games, imparting vitality to your mental acumen and making cognitive fitness an enjoyable endeavor.

Tips for some of the best brain game apps

The App Store boasts an extensive array of cognitive challenge applications, meticulously engineered to tantalize and fortify the faculties of the human mind. In this segment, we furnish invaluable counsel and commendations for handpicked cognitive challenge applications that distinguish themselves on the grounds of superlative quality.

Whether your aspiration revolves around memory enhancement, finesse in troubleshooting, or an elongated attention span, these applications represent a compelling amalgamation of amusement and efficacy. Our exploration encompasses the crème de la crème of cognitive challenge applications, embarking upon detailed analyses of their attributes, mechanisms of interaction, and the avenues through which they can enrich cognitive well-being.

From venerable classics such as Sudoku and cryptic crossword puzzles to avant-garde cognitive training applications, you will encounter a manifold selection tailored to your proclivities and aspirations. This section aspires to function as your guiding compass in the process of ascertaining the cognitive challenge applications most congruent with your objectives, propelling you toward sustained mental agility and unbridled engagement.

> *Pro Tip: Explore the vast pantheon of brain game apps gracing the App Store, embarking on a quest for applications that proffer a multifaceted array of challenges, targeting various facets of cognitive prowess.*

How to download and play games from the App Store

Engaging with cognitive challenge applications procured from the App Store is an intuitive and accessible endeavor. Nonetheless, this section endeavors to deliver an exhaustive compendium of procedural directives to ensure your inaugural strides transpire with seamless efficacy. From the inception of app perusal to the culminating juncture of app initiation, you will be furnished with comprehensive instructions, underpinning the entire journey of accessing these meritorious applications. Our elucidation encompasses a systematic sequence of actions, encompassing the pursuit of cognitive challenge applications, the secure installation thereof, and the inaugural activation of these digital assets.

This section proffers invaluable advisories concerning the art of configuration management, the meticulous oversight of performance metrics, and the maximization of your cognitive challenge undertaking. Upon traversing the contents of this guide, you will emerge with a profound comprehension and fortified assurance, poised to seamlessly integrate cognitive challenge engagements into your quotidian routine, thus ushering in contributions to your cognitive robustness and mental equilibrium.

> *Pro Tip: Navigate the realm of app selection with discernment, consulting user reviews and scrutinizing app ratings to ensure the adoption of high-quality, engaging options that align with your cognitive enhancement aspirations.*

Chapter 10:

Mobility, Travel, and Support

10.1 Maps and GPS

Using the Maps app: search for locations, get directions, and view in different modes (satellite, standard)

Maps

The Maps application nestled within your iPhone emerges as the quintessential tool for navigating your world. This section delves into the adept utilization of the Maps app, encompassing the exploration of locales, the acquisition of meticulously detailed route guidance for both vehicular and pedestrian movement, and the contemplation of diverse visual perspectives like the satellite and standard views.

Whether your aim entails planning an extended road sojourn or seeking out a proximate dining establishment, this manual empowers you to harness the complete gamut of capabilities conferred by the Maps app.

> *Pro Tip: Expedite access to directions, particularly during your daily commute, by saving your residence and workplace addresses within the Maps application.*

Traffic information and alternative routes

Maintaining an edge over traffic fluctuations stands as a prerogative, and the Maps app emerges as a paragon of virtue by providing current traffic statistics along with recommendations for alternative routes.

This section illuminates the procedures for accessing this feature, staying abreast of real-time traffic scenarios, and effecting judicious decisions while traversing the thoroughfares.

> *Pro Tip: Prior to commencing your journey, peruse traffic conditions and estimated arrival times. Maps can proffer alternative routes to circumvent potential delays.*

Find nearby points of interest

Facilitating the discovery of proximate points of interest assumes the aspect of simplicity personified through the Maps app. This section expounds upon the methodologies for locating dining establishments, refueling stations, automated teller machines, and other indispensable establishments situated in proximity to your existing coordinates.

Whether you're navigating unfamiliar urban landscapes or meandering through your hometown, your proximity to requisite amenities remains assured.

> *Pro Tip: Engage in a thorough exploration of your vicinity by conducting searches for proximate dining establishments, fuel stations, or attractions. Maps can supply ratings and reviews to facilitate judicious decision-making.*

Use Siri for voice-activated navigation

Siri emerges as your virtual copilot when it comes to navigational matters. This segment unravels the intricacies of invoking voice commands to elicit directions, pinpoint nearby establishments, or ascertain the prevailing traffic conditions without the need for manual intervention.

Siri's acumen in voice-activated navigation not only accentuates safety but also ushers in a dimension of convenience that remains unparalleled.

> *Pro Tip: While within the Maps application, activate Siri to facilitate hands-free navigation. Siri can be summoned to provide directions, conduct specific place searches, or deliver real-time traffic updates.*

10.2 Travel and transportation apps

Overview of popular travel apps: Booking.com, Airbnb, Uber, etc.

Embarking upon expeditions facilitated by esteemed applications like Booking.com, Airbnb, and Uber bestows upon you the keys to a realm of travel and transportation. This section proffers an introductory vista of these applications, thereby spotlighting their attributes and elucidating how they serve to streamline your odyssey. From securing accommodations to orchestrating vehicular conveyance, you shall unearth the manifold ways in which these applications enrich your sojourn.

> *Pro Tip: Diversify your array of travel applications to enable a comparative analysis of pricing and availability. Some applications may proffer exclusive discounts or incentives.*

How to make reservations, book flights, or rent a car using apps

The act of booking flights, reserving lodgings, and renting automobiles has evolved into a process marked by sheer simplicity through travel applications. This section imparts comprehensive guidance on the art of utilizing travel applications for the execution of reservations, encompassing tips and techniques for uncovering the most attractive bargains while ensuring the seamlessness of the booking procedure.

Manage and check travel itineraries

The preservation of a systematic record of your travel plans constitutes an imperative endeavor.

This section delineates the means by which you may manage and review your travel itineraries by means of travel applications. You'll be apprised of the mechanisms that permit access to your reservations, the examination of trip specifics, and the receipt of timely updates, thus ensuring that your sojourn remains a consummately organized and hassle-free affair.

Pro Tip: Simplify the organization of your travel itineraries by forwarding email confirmations to the Mail application on your iPhone, automatically generating and updating travel schedules within the "Trips" folder.

Local guides and recommendations based on current location

The undertaking of unraveling the treasures concealed within a novel destination unveils itself as a voyage of discovery, and travel applications, in turn, divulge local guides and bespoke recommendations harmonized with your present location.

This segment unravels how these applications provide insights into nearby attractions, dining havens, and leisure activities, allowing you to savor your peregrinations akin to a seasoned sojourner.

Pro Tip: Grant location access to your travel applications to facilitate the receipt of personalized recommendations and the unearthing of concealed gems while traversing new urban landscapes.

10.3 Support and accessibility features

Overview of built-in accessibility features: VoiceOver, magnification, larger text, etc.

Apple's unwavering commitment to accessibility finds its manifestation in the iPhone, which arrives endowed with a profusion of intrinsic features tailored to enhance accessibility.

This section acquaints you with a panoramic perspective of these features, encompassing the multifaceted utility of VoiceOver for the auditory rendering of on-screen content, magnification's role in affording visual assistance, and the customization options pertaining to enlarged text. It stands as a guide ensuring that your iPhone stands configured to cater to your distinct accessibility requisites.

Pro Tip: Tailor accessibility features to align with your unique requisites. Customize text dimensions, activate color filtration, or establish voice-activated commands for an optimized user experience.

Adjust settings for vision, hearing, motor, and learning

The calibration of your iPhone's settings to mirror your singular requisites stands as a cornerstone of accessibility.

This section expounds upon the methodologies for the fine-tuning of settings geared towards addressing the spectrum of accessibility exigencies, spanning vision, hearing, motor, and learning assistance requirements.

Whether you seek text of an enlarged scale, closed captions for audio-visual content, or voice-driven interactions, you shall be duly equipped with stepwise directives for optimizing your iPhone's accessibility attributes.

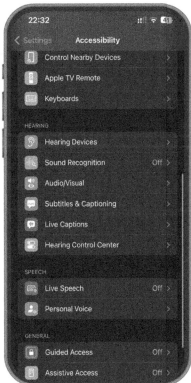

Pro Tip: Engage in a comprehensive exploration of the "Accessibility" settings to unveil features that can amplify your iPhone's functionality, attuned to your precise needs.

Use Siri for voice commands and dictation

Siri, the digital assistant, transcends the realm of quotidian tasks to stand as a robust accessibility tool. Unearth the nuances of employing Siri for the issuance of voice-based commands and dictation, simplifying your interactions with your iPhone.

Whether you aspire to dispatch messages, set reminders, or acquire information, these functions are now attainable through the medium of voice input, fostering a more inclusive and convenient user experience.

Pro Tip: Master the spectrum of voice commands wielded by Siri to execute tasks with heightened efficiency, spanning from message transmission to reminder configuration, all sans the need for manual keystrokes or taps.

Find local Apple stores or authorized service providers

When the need arises for support or guidance concerning your Apple devices, this section elucidates the methodologies for ascertaining the proximity of local Apple stores or authorized service providers.

Whether confronted with technical quandaries or merely seeking the counsel of experts, possessing knowledge regarding the identification of sources of assistance becomes a prerogative, and this guide guarantees your preparedness in this regard.

Pro Tip: Prior to seeking support, peruse the Apple Support application to schedule appointments or pinpoint nearby service providers. This approach can conserve time and streamline the quest for the most conveniently situated assistance.

Chapter 11:

Recommended Third-Party Apps 🎤

(Essential for your iPhone)

11.1 Productivity

Evernote:

Evernote, an omnipresent note-taking app, stands as the veritable bedrock of productivity for a global user base. It proffers an all-encompassing ecosystem for the meticulous orchestration of your digital realm. Evernote empowers you to craft, administer, and synchronize notes, to-do lists, and reminders seamlessly across a plethora of devices.

Adorned with features like tags, notebooks, and an advanced search paradigm, it bestows the gift of immaculate digital organization, always at your beck and call. Irrespective of whether you're encapsulating nascent ideas, chronicling meeting deliberations, or preserving web clippings, Evernote ascends to the status of an indispensable instrument for nurturing structured efficacy and unwavering productivity.

> *Pro Tip: Initiate the creation of distinct notebooks within Evernote for specific projects or categories, thereby fostering meticulous organization and expeditious accessibility of your notes. Employ tags as an additional layer of classification for your notes, facilitating efficient retrieval.*

Microsoft Office (Word, Excel, PowerPoint):

Microsoft Office applications extend the omnipotence of the world's most exalted productivity software to the confines of your iPhone. These applications, encompassing Word, Excel, and PowerPoint, consociate to deliver a familiar and potent arsenal of utilities for sundry tasks. Be it the composition of documents, the curation of intricate spreadsheets, or the conception of captivating presentations, Microsoft Office stands as your bastion of creative and organizational empowerment.

The seamlessness of these applications' integration with cloud services such as OneDrive ensures

the perennial accessibility of your work, even when traversing the realms of mobility. Whether harnessed for personal endeavors or professional pursuits, Microsoft Office applications constitute an indelible facet of the iPhone experience, hinged on the tenets of productivity maximization.

> *Pro Tip: Enable the auto-save functionality within Microsoft Office applications to ensure the perpetual preservation of your work, consequently mitigating the risk of inadvertent document loss.*

Dropbox:

Dropbox transcends the contours of mere cloud storage, emerging as an epicenter for the sharing and archiving of digital artifacts in this epoch of virtuality.

With Dropbox, the synchronization of your files across a sundry array of devices becomes an endeavor bereft of impediments. Gone are the days of laborious endeavors involving the mailing of documents to oneself or the cumbrous transportation of corporeal records.

Dropbox confers convenience par excellence, whether the objective entails collaborative efforts with peers, the facile exchange of voluminous files, or the instantaneous access to your dossier while treading uncharted terrain.

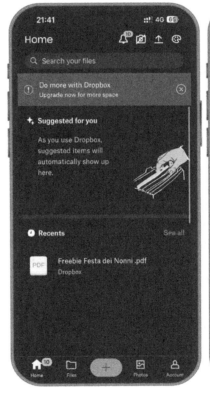 

DROPBOX   **WORD**

Dropbox also shines through the prism of its intuitive interface, further augmented by an entente cordiale with sundry other applications, thereby acquiring the status of an integral component of your operational framework. For the classification, sharing, and collaborative annotation of files, Dropbox emerges as a sine qua non, harmonizing the nuances of your digital sojourn.

> *Pro Tip: Harness Dropbox's file version history feature to restore prior iterations of a file, particularly beneficial when engaged in collaborative document editing.*

11.2 Communication

WhatsApp:

WhatsApp is a ubiquitous name in the realm of instant messaging, renowned for offering a secure and convenient conduit for maintaining connections with friends, family, and colleagues.

Through WhatsApp's multifaceted platform, you can seamlessly dispatch text messages, engage in voice and video calls, disseminate photos and videos, and orchestrate group chats.

Its impenetrable end-to-end encryption casts a protective veil over your messages, cultivating an atmosphere of privacy and security.

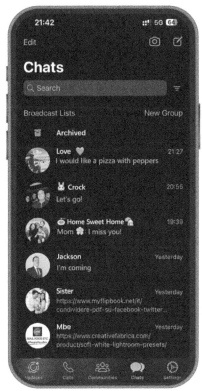

WHATSAPP

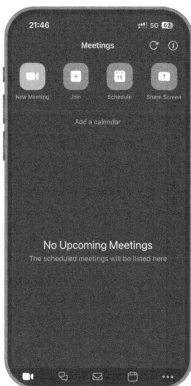

ZOOM

WhatsApp's platform agnosticism further solidifies its standing, facilitating interoperability across diverse devices and rendering it an exquisite choice for both personal and professional correspondence.

> *Pro Tip: Enhance the security of your WhatsApp conversations by activating two-step verification within the app's settings, augmenting the safeguarding of your account.*

Zoom:

In an age of escalating interconnectivity, Zoom has ascended as the quintessential vanguard in the realm of virtual meetings and video conferencing. Its mettle shines through as it furnishes a dependable platform for conducting webinars, orchestrating virtual meetings, and nurturing online collaboration.

Zoom's user-friendly interface and robust features render it indispensable, whether the endeavor entails business meetings or convivial gatherings with friends and family. With provisions for screen sharing, breakout rooms, and meeting recording, Zoom metamorphoses into a versatile instrument catering to the gamut of casual and professional communication.

Pro Tip: Prior to joining a Zoom meeting, undertake a preliminary assessment of your audio and video settings to ensure a seamless and hassle-free virtual meeting experience.

Skype:

Skype has perennially occupied the zenith of international communication platforms, proffering voice and video calling, instantaneous messaging, and the capability for group video conferencing. Its protean nature renders it the epitome for staying tethered with acquaintances scattered across the global tapestry, or convening remote business assemblies. Augmented by features such as call recording, screen sharing, and real-time language translation, Skype undergoes a continual evolution to cater to the eclectic demands of its diverse user base.

Pro Tip: Implement call forwarding settings in Skype to divert calls to an alternative number or voicemail, assuring that vital calls are never missed, even during offline periods.

11.3 Health and Wellness

MyFitnessPal:

MyFitnessPal emerges as the preeminent compatriot in your pursuit of fitness and nutritional excellence. Whether your objectives encompass weight loss, muscle gain, or the cultivation of a salubrious lifestyle, this app stands as the paragon of holistic guidance.

It empowers you to meticulously monitor your dietary consumption, log physical exertions, and establish fitness milestones. MyFitnessPal's expansive alimentary database expedites the process of scrutinizing your calorific intake and propounds a compendium of erudition for discerning dietary choices.

Furthermore, its harmonious synchronization with diverse fitness wearables ushers in an era of comprehensive health and wellness oversight.

Pro Tip: Exploit MyFitnessPal's barcode scanning feature as an expedited means to log food items, simplifying the tracking of your daily nutritional intake.

MY FITNESS PAL

Headspace:

Amidst the ceaseless hustle and bustle of contemporary existence, the cultivation of moments suffused with tranquility and relaxation assumes paramount significance. Headspace, the meditation and mindfulness app, serves as your beacon in this pursuit. It orchestrates an array of meditation and relaxation techniques, guiding you towards stress reduction, enhanced concentration, and superior sleep quality.

Endowed with a plethora of programs designed to inure against stress, optimize focus, and elevate sleep patterns, Headspace affords you the agency to steer your mental well-being. Its mellifluous voice-guided sessions demystify the practice of mindfulness, rendering it accessible to practitioners of all proficiencies, thereby ensconcing itself as an optimal choice for those aspiring to incorporate mindfulness regimens into their daily routines.

Pro Tip: Foster a consistent meditation regimen by earmarking a specific daily time slot for Headspace sessions, recognizing that regularity can amplify the benefits derived from meditation.

Pill Reminder:

The labyrinthine realm of medication management assumes a semblance of simplicity through the Pill Reminder app. This application obviates the challenges associated with adhering to medication regimens by dispatching punctilious reminders and notifications.

You possess the liberty to configure bespoke medication schedules, meticulously chronicle your pill consumption, and even procure refilling prompts. The Pill Reminder app stands as an impervious bulwark against missed doses, facilitating the preservation of your health and well-being with consummate ease.

Pro Tip: Personalize medication reminders with specific directives, such as stipulating whether pills should be taken with food or prior to bedtime, mitigating the likelihood of dosing errors.

11.4 Information and Reading

Kindle:

The Kindle app emerges as the book aficionado's quintessential companion. Whether you traverse the realms of voracious reading or indulge sporadically in literary pursuits, this app provides unfettered access to a vast repository of e-books and textual documents, all within the confines of your iPhone.

It grants you the latitude to procure and download books directly from the Amazon repository, permitting a tailored reading experience with adjustable fonts and thematic aesthetics. Moreover, the app facilitates the synchronization of your reading progress across a panoply of devices, making it an ideal choice for voracious readers on the move.

> *Pro Tip: Actively engage with your Kindle e-books by highlighting key passages and crafting annotations to facilitate interaction with the text and the convenient review of critical takeaways.*

Audible:

For those with an auditory inclination, Audible unfurls a veritable cornucopia of audiobooks and audio content.

With an eclectic array of literary genres at your disposal, encompassing bestsellers, literary classics, and self-improvement tomes, Audible transmutes your daily commute, workout routine, or leisure hours into immersive auditory odysseys.

The app extends the privilege of downloading audiobooks for offline auditions and the adjustment of playback velocity to align with your auditory proclivity. Whether you find yourself multitasking or simply yearn for an indulgent sonic escapade, Audible satiates your desires.

AUDIBLE

KINDLE

> *Pro Tip: Tailor the playback speed within Audible to conform to your preferred pace, enabling a comfortable and customizable audiobook listening experience.*

Feedly:

Navigating the labyrinthine landscape of contemporary news and blog content can be an arduous endeavor. Yet, Feedly endeavors to streamline this process by serving as a comprehensive news aggregator. It empowers you to track your cherished blogs, websites, and news outlets from

a singular vantage point. The app allows for the configuration of a bespoke newsfeed, the archiving of articles for perusal at your leisure, and the seamless facilitation of content sharing with acquaintances. With its user-intuitive interface and robust organizational features, Feedly crystallizes into an indispensable instrument for staying abreast of current affairs and maintaining relevance on topics that resonate with you.

Pro Tip: Optimize your reading experience by categorizing your Feedly subscriptions, affording streamlined access to topics of personal interest.

11.5 Entertainment

Spotify:

Spotify represents a paradisiacal haven for ardent music aficionados. This music streaming application bequeaths unrestricted entry to an expansive compendium of melodies, albums, and curated playlists spanning diverse musical genres and artists.

It endows you with the capacity to craft bespoke playlists, unravel novel musical discoveries through handpicked compilations, and effectuate song downloads for offline auditory gratification. While the free iteration of Spotify endows a plethora of features, its premium counterpart proffers the elimination of intrusive advertisements and unlocks supplementary amenities such as boundless track skipping and offline auditory engagement.

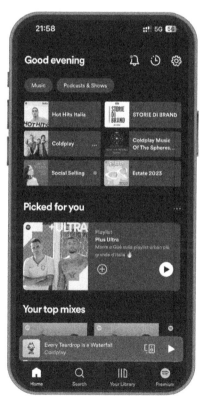

Regardless of whether you identify as a passionate music enthusiast or merely crave a harmonious backdrop to life's proceedings, Spotify caters to your auditory predilections.

Pro Tip: Create personalized playlists on Spotify that cater to diverse moods or activities, heightening the enjoyment of music exploration and discovery.

SPOTIFY

Netflix:

In the realm of streaming cinematic gems and episodic tapestries, Netflix emerges as a venerable household name.

A subscription to this platform confers access to an extensive vault of audiovisual content, encompassing award-worthy original series and celluloid masterpieces.

Netflix's user-friendly interface expedites the exploration of new titles, seamless resumption of previously viewed episodes, and the proposition of downloadable content for offline consumption, a boon for peripatetic souls or those ensconced in regions with suboptimal internet connectivity.

Pro Tip: Institute parental controls within Netflix to impose content restrictions based on age ratings, thereby ensuring a secure viewing environment for all family members.

NETFLIX

GOODREADS

Goodreads:

For the bibliophiles among us, Goodreads unfolds as an online sanctuary. This social networking platform serves as a crucible where literature aficionados unite to unearth, appraise, and critique books. It grants you the prerogative to assemble virtual bookshelves for the meticulous curation of your reading repertoire, provides an avenue to partake in book clubs, and encourages camaraderie amongst fellow bibliophiles.

Goodreads assumes the role of an omniscient bibliophile's ally by facilitating the serendipitous discovery of literary works aligned with your predilections, all while cultivating a communal space for impassioned literary dialogues. Whether your quest is to unearth book recommendations or proffer cogent analyses of your recent literary conquests, Goodreads furnishes a dynamic community of like-minded reading enthusiasts.

Pro Tip: Participate in book clubs and reading challenges within Goodreads to foster connections with fellow bibliophiles and diversify your reading repertoire.

11.6 Travel and Navigation

Google Maps:

While Apple Maps stands as the default cartographic option for iPhones, Google Maps emerges as a robust alternative, furnishing an arsenal of navigation tools. It dispenses intricate maps, real-time traffic intelligence, and detailed turn-by-turn route elucidation.

Google Maps excels in unveiling nearby points of interest, restaurants, and local enterprises, further bolstered by the immersive Street View feature, which provides visual previews of your intended destinations.

Additionally, the app proffers the ability to predownload maps for offline navigation, a godsend in regions devoid of stable internet connectivity.

> *Pro Tip: Save offline maps for frequently visited locales within Google Maps to navigate devoid of mobile data usage, proving invaluable during travels or in areas with weak signal reception.*

GOOGLE MAPS　　　　**TRIPADVISOR**

TripAdvisor:

When it comes to orchestrating voyages, TripAdvisor reigns as an invaluable compass. It furnishes a compendium of user-generated reviews and ratings pertaining to lodgings, dining establishments, and tourist attractions dispersed across the global canvas.

Whether your quest entails the quest for commendable hotels, the sifting of culinary critiques, or the absorption of travel advice, TripAdvisor unfurls a treasure trove of information bequeathed by fellow voyagers. Moreover, the application streamlines your journey planning process by proffering the facility to book accommodations and dining venues directly, thereby consolidating itself as a one-stop-shop for travel planning.

Pro Tip: Contribute to the TripAdvisor community by furnishing comprehensive reviews and ratings for establishments you patronize, thus aiding fellow travelers in making informed decisions.

Uber:

For seamless and dependable mobility, Uber takes the pole position as the quintessential travel companion. This application engenders direct connections with local drivers, simplifying the requisitioning of transportation for an array of travel exigencies. It allows you to monitor the real-time progress of your driver's approach, facilitates secure in-app payments, and invites you to furnish feedback by rating your overall travel experience. Uber's expansive footprint encompasses a plethora of cities worldwide, rendering it a convenient recourse for traversing from point A to point B.

Pro Tip: Set up multiple payment methods within the Uber app, encompassing credit cards and PayPal, to furnish payment flexibility when availing ride services.

11.7 Finance and Shopping

Mint:

Prudent financial stewardship constitutes a paramount endeavor, and Mint stands as an adept ally in this endeavor. It serves as an all-encompassing personal finance application, wielding the capacity to scrutinize your expenditures, establish fiscal thresholds, and oversee your financial well-being. Mint boasts automated transaction categorization, proffering insights into your monetary habits and dispatching reminders regarding impending bills. With all your fiscal data centralized, you're poised to render well-informed financial determinations.

Pro Tip: Create budgetary categories within Mint to meticulously track designated expenditures, encompassing categories like groceries, entertainment, or transportation, thereby facilitating enhanced financial management.

PayPal:

As a venerated bastion of online payment protocols, PayPal demystifies financial transactions and fund transfers. Whether your intent revolves around online shopping, fund remittances to acquaintances, or service remunerations, PayPal provides a secure and streamlined conduit for conducting monetary transactions.

The application extends the privilege of affixing your bank accounts or credit cards, thereby expediting seamless financial transactions.

Furthermore, PayPal's fortification via buyer and seller protection policies engenders tranquility when consummating online acquisitions or executing item venditions.

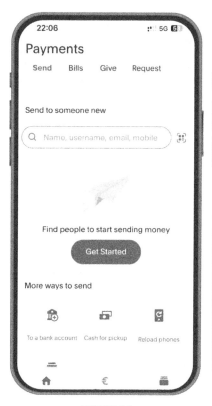

PAYPAL

AMAZON

Pro Tip: Fortify the security of your PayPal account by activating two-factor authentication (2FA), thereby erecting an additional bulwark to protect your financial data.

Amazon:

The Amazon application serves as a portal to an expansive digital marketplace. It transcends the realm of product procurement by endowing access to ancillary services, including Amazon Prime Video and Amazon Music (in cases of active subscriptions).

You're presented with the opportunity to peruse an aggregate myriad of merchandise, assimilate product critiques, and expedite acquisitions via a few deft screen touches. The application furthers the convenience quotient by proffering features such as one-click procurement and package tracking, rendering it a veritable retail juggernaut within the palm of your hand.

Pro Tip: Explore Amazon's "Deals" section to unearth discounted products and limited-time offers, optimizing your shopping experience.

11.8 Health and Fitness

MyFitnessPal:

In the quest for health and fitness optimization, MyFitnessPal constitutes a stalwart companion. It commences by empowering you to log and monitor your dietary intake, assuring that you stay attuned to your nutritional goals.

MyFitnessPal's extensive food database streamlines the process of recording meals, while its barcode scanner facilitates quick entry of packaged food details.

Furthermore, the application accommodates workout tracking, enabling you to record and analyze your physical exertions, fostering holistic health management.

> *Pro Tip: Connect MyFitnessPal with wearable fitness devices or other fitness apps to synchronize your exercise data seamlessly, providing comprehensive health insights.*

MY FITNESS PAL

Calm:

Amid the cacophonous exigencies of modern life, finding moments of reprieve and tranquility is imperative. Calm serves as a portal to serenity, offering guided meditation sessions, sleep stories, and relaxation exercises.

It empowers you to alleviate stress, cultivate mindfulness, and embark on a restorative journey to attain mental equilibrium. The application's intuitive interface and diverse meditation programs cater to individuals ranging from novices to seasoned practitioners.

> *Pro Tip: Incorporate Calm's meditation sessions into your daily routine, designating specific moments for mindfulness to enhance mental well-being.*

11.9 15+ Recommended Apps for Seniors:

1. Lumosity (brain games):

Lumosity assembles an array of cerebral exercises devised to augment memory, attention, and problem-solving proficiencies.

It serves as an engaging conduit for seniors striving to keep their cognitive faculties agile.

> *Pro Tip: Dedicate a few minutes each day to Lumosity's brain games to boost cognitive function and memory.*

2. AARP (senior resources):

The AARP application aggregates a wealth of resources, spanning articles, utilities, and discounts, all meticulously curated to cater to the requirements and inclinations of seniors.

> *Pro Tip: Explore the AARP app for valuable resources on health, finance, and lifestyle tailored to seniors.*

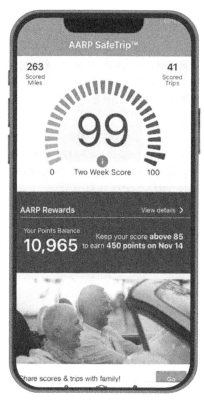

AARP

3. Medisafe (medication reminders):

Medication management poses a challenge for many seniors, yet Medisafe simplifies this process. The application disseminates timely reminders and notifications, aiding seniors in adhering to prescribed medication schedules.

> *Pro Tip: Use Medisafe to set medication reminders, ensuring you never miss a dose.*

4. Peak (memory and attention games):

Peak, akin to Lumosity, proffers an assortment of mental challenges designed to nurture cognitive acumen.

> *Pro Tip: Challenge yourself with Peak's memory and attention exercises to keep your mind sharp.*

5. Magnifying Glass (digital magnifying tool):

This application effectively transforms your iPhone into a digital magnifying glass, rendering small text legible and fine details perceptible, easing the ocular strain experienced by seniors.

> *Pro Tip: Use the Magnifying Glass app to zoom in on small text or objects for enhanced visibility.*

6. Words With Friends (word game):

A stimulating word puzzle game that fosters mental engagement and leisurely amusement.

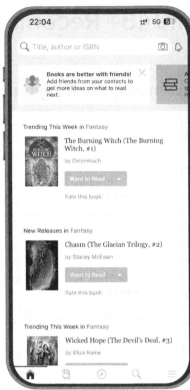

WORDS WITH FRIENDS   **GOOD READS**

> *Pro Tip: Stay mentally active by playing Words With Friends, a word game that fosters creativity and vocabulary*

7. Goodreads (reader community):

Goodreads constitutes a communal nexus for readers to unearth and discuss literary gems, thereby cultivating a sense of camaraderie amidst book enthusiasts.

> *Pro Tip: Join the Goodreads community to discover new books, share reading experiences, and find personalized book recommendations.*

8. Duolingo (language learning):

Embarking on the journey of learning a new language is an excellent cognitive exercise for seniors, and Duolingo extends a user-friendly avenue to achieve this goal.

> *Pro Tip: Learn a new language with Duolingo's bite-sized lessons and interactive exercises.*

9. Day One (digital journal):

Seniors can employ Day One for the purpose of journaling, chronicling memories, and contemplative retrospection.

Pro Tip: Start journaling with Day One to capture and cherish your life's memories and stories.

10. Weather Underground (comprehensive weather information):

Stay apprised of the meteorological conditions in your vicinity via Weather Underground's detailed forecasts.

Pro Tip: Stay informed about weather conditions and forecasts in your area with Weather Underground.

11. Pocket (article saving for later):

Pocket serves as an invaluable tool for archiving articles and web content for subsequent perusal.

Pro Tip: Use Pocket to save interesting articles and read them at your leisure, even offline.

SILVER SNEAKERS GO

12. SilverSneakers GO (senior fitness):

SilverSneakers GO delivers tailored workout routines and fitness guidance calibrated to the needs of seniors.

Pro Tip: Stay active with SilverSneakers GO, which offers fitness routines tailored to seniors' needs and abilities.

13. Brainwell (memory and attention exercises):

This application offers an eclectic array of exercises poised to stimulate memory and cognitive faculties among seniors.

Pro Tip: Incorporate Brainwell's memory and attention exercises into your daily routine to boost mental agility.

14. Elevate (mental conditioning): E

levate lays forth a series of daily brain-training exercises conceived to amplify mental agility and prowess.

> *Pro Tip: Elevate offers personalized brain training exercises to enhance your critical thinking and communication skills.*

15. My Pillbox (medication management):

My Pillbox stands as another application expressly engineered to facilitate medication management among seniors, ensuring seamless adherence to prescribed regimens and the preservation of well-being.

> *Pro Tip: Use My Pillbox to organize and manage your medications, ensuring your health and well-being.*

These recommendations for third-party applications span an extensive gamut of interests and requisites, thereby ensuring iPhone users can augment their productivity, communication, health, leisure, and more. Regardless of whether one identifies as a student, professional, senior, or simply an individual aiming to harness the iPhone's full potential, these applications furnish a plenitude of invaluable features and functionalities.

Chapter 12:

Tips and Tricks Section 🎤

12.1 - 15 Pro Tips and Tricks:

Using 3D Touch or Haptic Touch

The sphere of 3D Touch and Haptic Touch introduces a paradigm shift in iPhone interaction, imbuing it with heightened levels of engagement. **For those fortunate enough to possess devices that support 3D Touch, the capability to exert varying levels of pressure upon the screen unfolds an array of quick actions and previews.**

To illustrate, an assertive press upon the Camera app icon expedites the transition to capturing selfies or initiating video recordings. Devices featuring Haptic Touch, exemplified by the iPhone XR and subsequent iterations, mirror this functionality through prolonged presses, thereby extending the spectrum of swift actions. These attributes usher in a new era of efficiency, curtailing the number of steps requisite for the execution of commonplace tasks.

> *Pro Tip: Personalize your 3D Touch or Haptic Touch configurations in "Accessibility" to fine-tune the sensitivity, ensuring a more tailored experience.*

Creating Siri Shortcuts

Siri Shortcuts, a formidable asset within the iPhone arsenal, empowers users to automate multifarious tasks by crafting custom voice commands or engaging with shortcuts. The sheer potency of this tool becomes evident as it systematically streamlines one's digital milieu. Consider the prospect of engineering a shortcut denominated "Voyage Homeward."

When activated, this command orchestrates a cascade of actions that encompasses directional guidance, thermostatic home adjustments, and the dispatching of familial notifications, all elicited by a solitary utterance.

The adaptability of Siri Shortcuts, marked by a capacity for meticulous tailoring, metamorphoses the iPhone into a genuinely personal assistant, one that astutely anticipates and addresses your unique requisites.

> *Pro Tip: Develop Siri Shortcuts for routine tasks like dispatching messages to loved ones or initiating a specific playlist. This streamlines your daily routines efficiently.*

Using "Do Not Disturb While Driving"

The paramount imperative of safety while traversing the thoroughfares crystallizes through the advent of **"Do Not Disturb While Driving."** This feature, activated proactively, interfaces with your environment to discern motion within a vehicular context, subsequently relegating incoming calls, messages, and notifications into a muted state. Additionally, it proffers the ability to configure auto-reply missives designed for your contacts, succinctly apprising them of your en route status and pledging future correspondence. Such a mechanism epitomizes a proactive approach to distraction mitigation during vehicular navigation, culminating in the enhancement of not just your personal safety but the safety of fellow commuters.

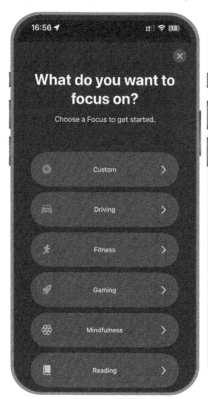

> *Pro Tip: Activate "Do Not Disturb While Driving" in settings to curtail distractions and advocate safe driving. Incoming calls and notifications will be automatically muted.*

Managing passwords with iCloud Keychain

The vanguard of password management within the Apple ecosystem, iCloud Keychain, orchestrates the symphony of a streamlined online existence in tandem with elevated security fortifications. It undertakes the impregnable safekeeping of your usernames, passwords, and credit card credentials across the pantheon of Apple devices, concomitantly simplifying your ingress into websites and applications.

The superlative functionality of iCloud Keychain further unfurls in the generation of robust, distinctive passwords for your digital accounts, adroitly auto-populating these credentials when requisite. This engenders a haven not only against the rigors of memory but against the insidious threat of password repetition, thereby fortifying the citadel of your online security.

> *Pro Tip: Periodically review and refresh your stored passwords in iCloud Keychain to uphold the security of your online accounts.*

Creating animated GIFs with Live Photos

Live Photos, capable of capturing fleeting moments of dynamism alongside static imagery, constitute the substratum for the effervescent realm of animated GIFs. This facile transformation grants an effulgent aura to your photographic repertoire, infusing creativity and vivacity.

Picture the metamorphosis of a Live Photo encapsulating a dear friend's candle-extinguishing ritual during a birthday celebration into an enchanting GIF, poised for dissemination among kith and kin. The potentiality is inexhaustible, breathing vitality into your recollections and rendering them available for dissemination in an interactive and captivating manner.

> *Pro Tip: Transform Live Photos into lively GIFs and share them with friends, infusing your messaging interactions with fun and dynamism.*

Quick settings through the Control Center

The Control Center stands as the fulcrum of command, a bastion of elemental settings and functionalities poised at your fingertips. A cursory swipe unearths its pantheon, facilitating the expeditious adjustment of parameters such as Wi-Fi, Bluetooth, screen luminosity, and more.

The verdant pastures of the Control Center's allure lie in its bespoke configuration, affording you the privilege of cherry-picking the

CONTROL CENTER

controls that hold pertinence to your unique purview. This personalized tapestry ensures that your frequently engaged functions linger a mere swipe away, ameliorating quotidian operations and mitigating the need for labyrinthine navigation across disparate settings interfaces.

Pro Tip: Tailor your Control Center by adding or removing shortcuts to your frequently employed functions for swift access.

Scanning documents with the Notes app

The Notes app, a linchpin of digital notetaking, unveils a kaleidoscope of capabilities far surpassing the rudiments of its titular function.

One beacon feature amongst the constellation is document scanning, a wondrous facet facilitated by your iPhone's camera.

It permits the seamless conversion of corporeal documents, inclusive of receipts, handwritten musings, or any parchment-based materials, into pristine digital PDF incarnations.

This exalted feature charts a course for document administration in the digital realm, curbing physical clutter through the judicious

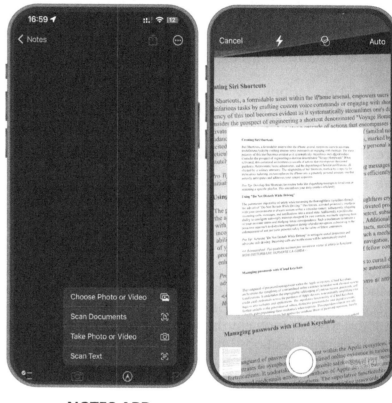

NOTES APP

digitization of consequential papers. Whether it pertains to the meticulous archiving of receipts, the guardianship of vital documents, or the expeditious information dissemination, this feature stands as a paragon of practicality.

Pro Tip: Harness the Notes app's document scanning capability to convert physical documents, receipts, and handwritten notes into digital formats for effortless organization and sharing.

Customizing widgets on the Home screen

Widgets, dynamic chalices of information graced with apposite tidbits from your cherished applications, engender an epochal metamorphosis of your Home screen, bestowing upon it the sylvan mien of personalization and informational supremacy.

With iOS 17 and its progeny in tow, your Home screen evolves into a canvas rife with creative interpretation, where widgets, encompassing a menagerie of insights like forthcoming calendar soirees, meteorological conjecture, or nascent communiqués, may be intricately tailored to satiate your craving for pertinent knowledge.

This technological tapestry galvanizes productivity, by endowing you with instant access to updates bereft of the necessity to traverse the labyrinthine thoroughfare of application accession, instead, manifesting essential information in seamless proximity.

> *Pro Tip: Customize your Home screen with widgets that display pertinent information at a glance, such as weather updates, calendar events, or current news headlines.*

Using "Dark Mode" for visual comfort

"Dark Mode," a diurnal counterpart of visual regalement, transfigures the chromatic schema of your iPhone's interface, shrouding it in the obsidian vestments of obscurity. Beneath its sartorial elegance, "Dark Mode" proffers pragmaticity in generous proportions.

It navigates the labyrinth of ocular fatigue, particularly amidst the languid ambience of diminished illumination, by mitigating the outflow of the notorious blue light, a nocturnal nemesis to tranquil slumber.

For devices boasting OLED displays, such as the iPhone X and their progeny, "Dark Mode" serves as a beacon of fiscal acumen, preserving battery life by dint of OLED displays' intrinsic predisposition toward energy thrift in the presence of inky hues. Activation of this mode is executed as effortlessly as the toggling of a switch, thereby championing a dual mandate of aesthetics and energy-conscious comfort.

Pro Tip: Activate Dark Mode during nighttime or in low-light environments to reduce eye strain and conserve OLED display battery life.

Syncing photos with iCloud

The iCloud Photo Library, a sanctified repository for your photographic corpus, starts a symphony of synchronization betwixt your Apple devices. Through its invocation, your cherished photographs and videos commence an ethereal sojourn into the vales of iCloud, ensconced in the cloud's omniscient embrace, rendering them accessible from any device that beseeches the blessings of your Apple ID.

This endows the expediency of liberation from the shackles of manual photo transference, concurrently endowing an impenetrable bastion of backup for your precious memories.

The vault of iCloud Photo Library is not content to merely house your recollections but adroitly executes the optimization of storage resources by relegating high-resolution imagery to the cloud's custody whilst preserving scaled-down iterations in localized precincts. This seamless confluence ensures perennial accessibility to your visual reminiscences, unfettered by considerations of the device in current employment.

Pro Tip: Configure iCloud Photos to seamlessly synchronize and access your photo collection across all your Apple devices, safeguarding your cherished memories.

Locking notes with Face ID or Touch ID

Privacy, a quintessential concern in the pantheon of iPhone user apprehensions, finds eloquent address through the medium of the Notes app. Herein, individual notes attain the zenith of security, aegis that encompasses both Face ID and Touch ID.

This additional stratum of security confers inviolability upon notes bearing sensitive or classified information. Contemplate the formulation of a locked note, clandestine custodian of critical login credentials, fiscal minutiae, or confidential ruminations. The mantle of exclusivity unfurled by this feature is such that sole access lies within your purview, irregardless of other individuals potentially wielding the key to your unlocked iPhone. This practical and expedient aspect of safeguarding privacy refrains from compromising convenience, thus bridging the chasm betwixt the paradigms of security and accessibility.

Pro Tip: Safeguard sensitive information by locking notes within the Notes app using Face ID or Touch ID, fortifying your privacy.

Setting up "Announce Messages with Siri"

"Announce Messages with Siri," a paradigmatic exemplar of connectivity and informedness in dynamic flux, unfurls its remit while you traverse the realms of mobility. With AirPods or their headphone compatriots, Siri ingeniously commandeers incoming missives, committing them to the realm of audibility and bequeathing you the prerogative of voice-driven riposte.

This hands-free modus operandi gains particular prominence during the execution of disparate activities, including but not confined to vehicular navigation, corporeal exertions, and multifaceted multitasking. This functionality, an oasis of accessibility, ensures that your operational cadence remains undisturbed by the imperative to physically engage with your iPhone in the quest for message elucidation.

The seamless confluence of Siri with your messaging apps galvanizes productivity and connectivity, thereby fostering a milieu replete with operational efficiency.

Pro Tip: Switch on this feature to have Siri audibly announce incoming messages, ensuring you stay connected while on the move without needing to check your device.

Quickly searching for apps using the Spotlight search bar

The Spotlight search bar, a paragon of iPhone utility, emerges as a veritable Excalibur for the unearthing of content enshrined within your iPhone. A mere swipe, precipitated by the downward traversal of your home screen or the direct summoning from any habitat, instantaneously activates an all-encompassing search initiative.

SPOTLIGHT

This initiative, with its unswerving pursuit of your quarry, starts a relentless quest for apps, contacts, messages, missives, communiqués, and documents. Its investigative prowess transcends nomenclatural confines, venturing deep into the heartland of content contained within apps and advancing the imputation of predictive prophecies.

As the preeminent chronicle in the annals of temporal conservation, this feature prunes the temporal expenditure that concomitantly burgeons in the presence of a plethora of apps and files, ensuring that your requisite discoveries arrive expeditiously and without the ceremonial rigors of manual navigation.

> *Pro Tip: Swipe down on your Home screen to reveal the Spotlight search bar; it's an expedient method for discovering and launching apps, contacting individuals, and more.*

Setting limits with "Screen Time"

In the epoch of contemporary digitality, the strategic choreography of screen time assumes paramount significance as a bulwark against the scourge of digital insularity. The venerated feature known as "Screen Time" emerges as the vanguard of this endeavor, expounding insights into your device deployment.

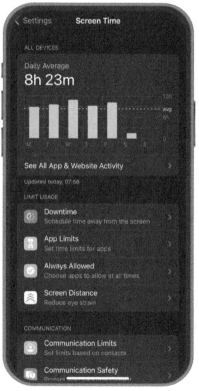

It articulates the extent of your interaction with specific apps and pursuits, unveiling a wealth of data pertaining to your digital ontology. "Screen Time" further invests you with the mantle of authority by way of daily allotments for app genres, orchestrated downtime intervals for abstention from digital realms, and a repository of detailed activity chronicles.

The strategic deployment of "Screen Time" equips you with the apparatus of self-regulation, poised to confront and subdue the specter of digital engulfment. In so doing, it aspires to transmute your iPhone into a catalyst for augmentation rather than subjugation, an emblem of mindful equilibrium within the cloisters of the digital age.

> *Pro Tip: Leverage Screen Time to establish app usage limits and scheduled downtime, promoting a harmonious balance between screen time and other activities.*

SCREEN TIME

The mastery of these Pro Tips and techniques unveils the profound potential latent within your iPhone. These features, though perhaps concealed beneath the veneer of conventionality, subsume a collective effervescence that augments efficiency, security, and personalization, thereby refining the entirety of your iPhone encounter. From the expedited streamlining of operations through the agency of Siri Shortcuts to the inviolable bastion of privacy via locked notes, these techniques bequeath empowerment for the realization of your device's fullest potential, ensuring its harmony with your specific desires and predilections.

Conclusion

In conclusion, the iPhone stands as an extraordinary contraption, bestowing upon its possessor an expansive array of functionalities meticulously engineered to streamline existence and elevate quotidian encounters. Throughout this exhaustive compendium, we have embarked on an intricate journey through the multifaceted domains of the iPhone's attributes and capabilities. These encompass its rudimentary functionalities, such as the initiation of voice communications and the dispatch of textual messages, extending to the deployment of advanced stratagems and stratagems that unlock its comprehensive potential.

Our journey started with an immersive plunge into the foundational strata, encompassing a plethora of aspects ranging from the induction of your iPhone's initiation and the adept navigation of its intricate interface to the adept administration of your contacts and telephonic conversations. Proficiency in harnessing quintessential tools such as the Camera application and the meticulously arranged Photos gallery not only serves to chronicle and immortalize cherished memories but also endows one with the demeanor of an adept and adroit iPhone adept.

Moreover, the exposé shepherded us into the domain of textual communication through the conduit of iMessage, an arena where one's expressive palette is significantly expanded through the utilization of emojis and the participation in convivial group dialogues. The art of location sharing, the engagement in FaceTime telecommunication sessions, and the beguiling exploration of terrestrial vistas by means of the Maps application all contributed to embellishing our perceptive apparatus.

Yet, the iPhone's role isn't merely circumscribed to that of a communication apparatus; it serves as a linchpin in our pursuit of sound health and robust well-being. Thus, we embarked upon an exploration of the multifarious facets that contribute to this sphere, including the Health application, its integral emergency features, and the nuances of configuring reminders for medicament ingestions and pivotal appointments. Concurrently, we cast our gaze upon the panorama of leisure activities, productivity pursuits, and the myriads of third-party applications, discovering how the iPhone is equipped to cater to an extensive spectrum of interests and imperatives.

Conclusively, our odyssey culminated in the revelation of a trove of advanced stratagems and stratagems capable of transmuting your iPhone into a bespoke implement of unparalleled personalization and operational efficiency. Attributes such as Siri Shortcuts, the "Do Not Disturb While Driving" protocol, and the meticulous stewardship of screen time ushered in an era where users can wrest control over their digital existences.

In an era where technology perpetually assumes an escalating role, the iPhone, a paragon of adaptability and innovation, continues to perpetuate its vanguard status in the echelons of modernity. Be you a neophyte iPhone custodian or a seasoned maven, this compendium furnishes you with the perspicacity and expertise essential to fathom the depths of your device, thereby facilitating the pursuit of seamless connectivity, organizational sagacity, and recreational solace whilst preserving the sanctum of privacy and security.

The iPhone, an entity in perpetual evolution, accompanied by an entourage of applications and accessories, transcends its mere status as an artifact; it metamorphoses into an enduring compeer that elevates existence and furnishes the navigators of the digital epoch with confidence and convenience. As you persist in the venture of scrutinizing and capitalizing on the manifold competences of your iPhone, novel avenues of facilitating life's rigors, augmenting its joys, and intensifying its connections will unfurl before you.

Index

Made in the USA
Las Vegas, NV
01 December 2023

81888591R00116